Vocabulary  GRADE 2
Fundamentals

Writing: Rachel Lynette
Content Editing: Marilyn Evans
Leslie Sorg
Copy Editing: Carrie Gwynne
Art Direction: Cheryl Puckett
Design/Production: Carolina Caird
Cover Design: Liliana Potigian

EMC 2802

EDUCATIONAL PUBLISHERS
Helping Children Learn since 1979

**Congratulations on your
purchase of some of the
finest teaching materials
in the world.**

*Photocopying the pages in this book
is permitted for <u>single-classroom use only</u>.
Making photocopies for additional classes
or schools is prohibited.*

For information about other Evan-Moor products, call 1-800-777-4362,
fax 1-800-777-4332, or visit our Web site, www.evan-moor.com.
Entire contents © 2010 EVAN-MOOR CORP.
18 Lower Ragsdale Drive, Monterey, CA 93940-5746.

Visit *teaching-standards.com* to view a
correlation of this book's activities to your
state's standards. This is a free service.

CPSIA: Bang Printing, 28210 N. Avenue Stanford, Valencia, CA 91355 [10/2009]

Contents

What's in *Vocabulary Fundamentals?*

Vocabulary Fundamentals provides leveled practice for essential vocabulary skills, reinforcing your core language arts program. Skills are presented in scaffolded three-page units, enabling you to target the varied learning needs within your classroom.

SKILL UNITS The core of *Vocabulary Fundamentals* is 42 three-page skill units. Each successive page in a unit increases in difficulty.

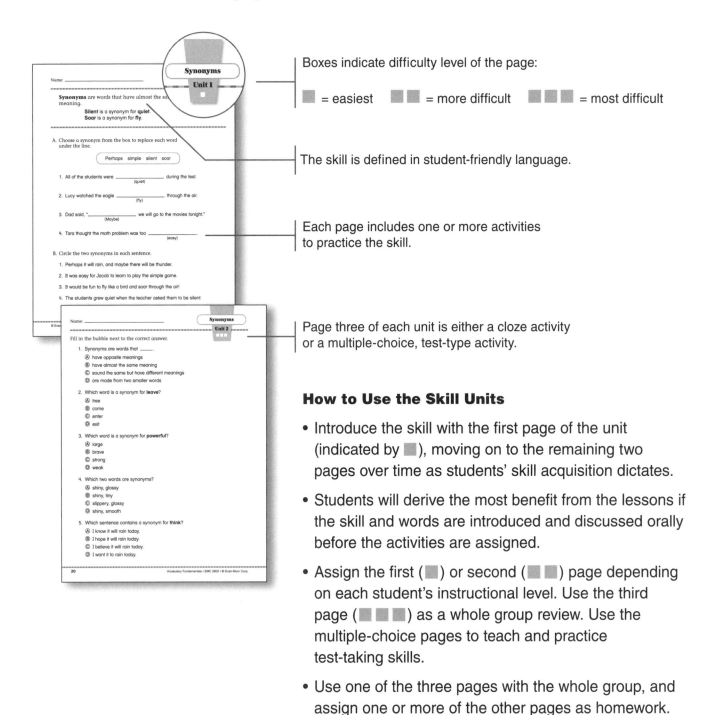

Boxes indicate difficulty level of the page:

■ = easiest   ■ ■ = more difficult   ■ ■ ■ = most difficult

The skill is defined in student-friendly language.

Each page includes one or more activities to practice the skill.

Page three of each unit is either a cloze activity or a multiple-choice, test-type activity.

How to Use the Skill Units

- Introduce the skill with the first page of the unit (indicated by ■), moving on to the remaining two pages over time as students' skill acquisition dictates.

- Students will derive the most benefit from the lessons if the skill and words are introduced and discussed orally before the activities are assigned.

- Assign the first (■) or second (■ ■) page depending on each student's instructional level. Use the third page (■ ■ ■) as a whole group review. Use the multiple-choice pages to teach and practice test-taking skills.

- Use one of the three pages with the whole group, and assign one or more of the other pages as homework.

WORD PLAY ACTIVITIES

Following the 42 skill units are 20 pages devoted to activities that build vocabulary in more creative, playful ways. Students will experience the fun of playing with words while expanding their vocabularies. Many of the word challenges presented encourage the use of critical-thinking skills.

How to Use the Word Play Pages

Use the Word Play pages for homework, as free-choice activities, at a language arts center, or as a change-of-pace activity for the whole group.

Integrating *Vocabulary Fundamentals* into Your Classroom

- Support reading comprehension by improving students' ability to determine word meaning through the use of context clues, recognition of familiar word parts, and word associations.

- Build students' writing vocabulary and reinforce skills such as choosing precise words and using descriptive language.

- Improve spelling by practicing strategies for recognizing word parts and phonic elements.

A **compound word** is a word made up of
two smaller words.

drive + way = **driveway**   bed + room = **bedroom**

A. Match two small words to make a compound word.

1. door   •   • plant

2. house   •   • shaker

3. fire   •   • bell

4. salt   •   • paper

5. news   •   • driver

6. screw   •   • place

B. Write each compound word from above under the correct picture.

A **compound word** is a word made up of two smaller words.

A. Circle the compound word in each sentence.
   Write the two smaller words that form each compound word.

1. The dishwasher is broken.   _____ + _____

2. The doorknob was sticky.   _____ + _____

3. Kate skipped down the hallway.   _____ + _____

4. Joe stood in the doorway.   _____ + _____

5. You can paint the bookshelf blue.   _____ + _____

6. Tim's bedroom is not very big.   _____ + _____

7. We played catch in the driveway.   _____ + _____

8. Mom is reading the newspaper.   _____ + _____

9. Did you water the houseplant?   _____ + _____

10. Our kitchen is downstairs.   _____ + _____

B. Complete each sentence with a compound word from above.

1. Sam's _____ is at the end of the hall.

2. Tonight it is Anna's turn to load the _____.

3. Jody went _____ to get a snack.

4. Jim reads the _____ every Sunday morning.

5. A _____ may need a lot of sunlight.

Name: _____

Fill in the bubble next to the correct answer.

1. Which word fits with **house** to make a compound word?

   Ⓐ chair

   Ⓑ paper

   Ⓒ plant

   Ⓓ room

2. Which word fits with **place** to make a compound word?

   Ⓐ our

   Ⓑ fire

   Ⓒ yard

   Ⓓ news

3. Which word does <u>not</u> fit with **way** to make a compound word?

   Ⓐ hall

   Ⓑ bath

   Ⓒ drive

   Ⓓ door

4. Which word is <u>not</u> a compound word?

   Ⓐ window

   Ⓑ bookshelf

   Ⓒ doorknob

   Ⓓ armchair

5. Which one is the proper way to divide **downstairs** into parts?

   Ⓐ downst | airs

   Ⓑ dow | nstairs

   Ⓒ downs | tairs

   Ⓓ down | stairs

Name: _____

A **compound word** is a word made up of
two smaller words.

grass + hopper = **grasshopper**   dragon + fly = **dragonfly**

A. Match two small words to make a compound word.

1. rattle   •   • bird

2. sword   •   • fly

3. humming •   • fish

4. earth   •   • bee

5. fire   •   • snake

6. honey   •   • worm

B. Use the two pictures in each box to make a compound word.

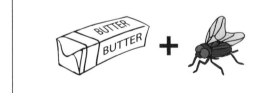

_____

_____

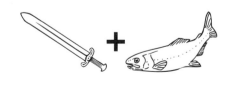

_____

_____

A **compound word** is a word made up of
two smaller words.

A. Circle the compound word in each group.
   Then write the two smaller words on the lines.

1. dragonfly   beetle   cricket   _____ + _____

2. lobster   walrus   jellyfish _____ + _____

3. bullfrog   lizard   turtle   _____ + _____

4. cobra   python   rattlesnake _____ + _____

5. swallow   chicken   hummingbird _____ + _____

6. honeybee   hornet   spider   _____ + _____

7. blackbird   eagle   pelican   _____ + _____

8. salmon   shark   swordfish _____ + _____

B. Use the compound words from above to answer the questions.

1. Which two animals live in the ocean?

   _____ and _____

2. Which two animals have six legs?

   _____ and _____

3. Which two animals have feathers?

   _____ and _____

Fill in the bubble next to the correct answer.

1. Which word fits with **jelly** to make a compound word?

   Ⓐ jam

   Ⓑ sandwich

   Ⓒ fish

   Ⓓ tree

2. Which word fits with **worm** to make a compound word?

   Ⓐ earth

   Ⓑ skinny

   Ⓒ dirt

   Ⓓ fried

3. Which word does <u>not</u> fit with **bird** to make a compound word?

   Ⓐ blue

   Ⓑ fly

   Ⓒ black

   Ⓓ humming

4. Which word is <u>not</u> a compound word?

   Ⓐ firefly

   Ⓑ rattlesnake

   Ⓒ honeybee

   Ⓓ elephant

5. Which one is the proper way to divide **bullfrog** into parts?

   Ⓐ bull | frog

   Ⓑ bul | lfrog

   Ⓒ bullf | rog

   Ⓓ bu | llfrog

A **compound word** is a word made up of
two smaller words.

note + book = **notebook**   lunch + box = **lunchbox**

A. Circle the compound word in each sentence.

1. The playground at my school has a big slide.

2. I am learning to type on the keyboard.

3. Maria's classroom is at the end of the hall.

4. Andy does his homework at the table.

5. It is a good idea to proofread your work.

B. Circle the small word in each group that can be added
to make a compound word. Write it on the line.

1. class _____   desk   mate   clock

2. back _____   pack   front   box

3. lunch _____   box   apple   hot

4. paper _____   write   page   back

5. _____ day   night   week   month

6. _____ mark   red   class   book

7. _____ room   bath   library   big

8. _____ book   long   note   heavy

Name: _____

A **compound word** is a word made up of
two smaller words.

A. Choose a compound word from the box to answer each clue.

> notebook   backpack   keyboard
> weekday   playground   proofread

1. where you go at recess   _____

2. a bag to carry your books   _____

3. what you type on at the computer   _____

4. not Saturday or Sunday   _____

5. to check your work for mistakes   _____

6. store your papers in this   _____

B. Use the small words in the box to make two compound words.
Then use each new word in a sentence.

> lunch   work   home   box

Compound words: _____ and _____

1. _____

_____

2. _____

_____

Name: _____

A **compound word** is a word made up of two smaller words.

Choose the best word for each blank.

> proofread   classroom   homework   bookmark
> paperback   backpack   classmate   playground

I got to school early today. I went out to the _____

to swing on the bars. I saw my _____ Anna on my way

there. She was sitting under a tree, reading a _____

book. When she saw me, she asked me to sit with her. She put a

_____ in her book so she would not lose her place.

We talked about the spelling _____ that the teacher

had given us yesterday. I thought it was hard, but Anna said it was easy for

her. She offered to _____ my work. I got my spelling

paper out of my _____ and gave it to Anna. She looked

it over and found a mistake. Luckily, I had a pencil so I could fix it. Then

the bell rang and we raced to our _____ .

Synonyms are words that have almost the same meaning.

Silent is a synonym for **quiet**.
Soar is a synonym for **fly**.

A. Choose a synonym from the box to replace each word under the line.

Perhaps   simple   silent   soar

1. All of the students were _____ during the test.
(quiet)

2. Lucy watched the eagle _____ through the air.
(fly)

3. Dad said, "_____ we will go to the movies tonight."
(Maybe)

4. Tara thought the math problem was too _____.
(easy)

B. Circle the two synonyms in each sentence.

1. Perhaps it will rain, and maybe there will be thunder.

2. It was easy for Jacob to learn to play the simple game.

3. It would be fun to fly like a bird and soar through the air!

4. The students grew quiet when the teacher asked them to be silent.

Synonyms are words that have almost the same meaning.

A. Choose the correct word for each blank.

perhaps   simple   silent   soar

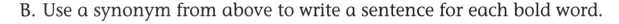

1. If you are quiet, you may be _____.

2. If a job is easy, it is _____.

3. Another word for **maybe** is _____.

4. When you fly, you _____ through the air.

B. Use a synonym from above to write a sentence for each bold word.

1. Write a sentence using a synonym for **fly**.

   _____

   _____

2. Write a sentence using a synonym for **simple**.

   _____

   _____

3. Write a sentence using a synonym for **quiet**.

   _____

   _____

Synonyms are words that have almost the same meaning.

Fill in each blank with the best synonym from the box.

quiet	fly	easy	maybe
silent	soar	simple	perhaps

Early this morning, my brother Anthony and I went to the park to

_____ our new kite. We were _____

as we tiptoed out the door. Once we got to the park, we took out the kite.

The kite had several pieces, but it was still _____ for

me to put it together. _____ it would have been

harder if my brother hadn't helped me.

When we got to the park, it was very _____.

I could not hear the wind at all. I worried that _____

there was not enough wind to fly the kite. We tried anyway. I held the

string, and my brother threw the kite into the air. It went up and up!

We watched it _____ high in the sky. Then I tried

a few _____ tricks. I made the kite dive and spin.

Soon, it was time to go. We wanted to get home for breakfast.

Dad was making chocolate chip pancakes!

Name: _____

Synonyms are words that have almost the same meaning.

> **Think** is a synonym for **believe**.
> **Strong** is a synonym for **powerful**.

A. Choose a synonym from the box to replace each word under the line.

> powerful   believe   glossy   exit

1. We will _____ when the movie is over.
   (leave)

2. I _____ it is your turn to do the dishes tonight.
   (think)

3. The _____ man lifted the heavy rock.
   (strong)

4. Hannah's new plastic purse is bright and _____.
   (shiny)

B. Fill in each blank with a word from the box.

1. **Leave** is a synonym for _____.

2. **Think** is a synonym for _____.

3. **Shiny** is a synonym for _____.

4. **Strong** is a synonym for _____.

Name: _____

Synonyms are words that have almost the same meaning.

A. Draw lines to match the synonyms.

1. exit   •   • shiny

2. believe   •   • leave

3. glossy   •   • strong

4. powerful •   • think

B. Use a synonym from above to write a sentence for each bold word.

1. Write a sentence using a synonym for **think**.

   _____

   _____

2. Write a sentence using a synonym for **strong**.

   _____

   _____

3. Write a sentence using a synonym for **shiny**.

   _____

   _____

4. Write a sentence using a synonym for **leave**.

   _____

   _____

Name: _____

Fill in the bubble next to the correct answer.

1. Synonyms are words that _____ .

   Ⓐ have opposite meanings

   Ⓑ have almost the same meaning

   Ⓒ sound the same but have different meanings

   Ⓓ are made from two smaller words

2. Which word is a synonym for **leave**?

   Ⓐ tree

   Ⓑ come

   Ⓒ enter

   Ⓓ exit

3. Which word is a synonym for **powerful**?

   Ⓐ large

   Ⓑ brave

   Ⓒ strong

   Ⓓ weak

4. Which two words are synonyms?

   Ⓐ shiny, glossy

   Ⓑ shiny, tiny

   Ⓒ slippery, glossy

   Ⓓ shiny, smooth

5. Which sentence contains a synonym for **think**?

   Ⓐ I know it will rain today.

   Ⓑ I hope it will rain today.

   Ⓒ I believe it will rain today.

   Ⓓ I want it to rain today.

Name: _____

Synonyms are words that have almost the same meaning.

Certain is a synonym for **sure**.
Weep is a synonym for **cry**.

A. Complete each sentence with a synonym from the box.

certain   weep   delete   nearly

1. The sad movie made Mara _____.
   (cry)

2. Colin wanted to _____ a misspelled word.
   (erase)

3. Tony was _____ he had shut the door.
   (sure)

4. Jade had _____ enough money for a train ticket.
   (almost)

B. Circle the two synonyms in each sentence.

1. Nathan is nearly four feet tall and weighs almost eighty pounds.

2. Sarah started to weep when she saw her little sister cry.

3. Sam wasn't sure he knew the way, but I was certain that I did.

Name: _____

Synonyms are words that have almost the same meaning.

Rewrite each sentence. Use a synonym from the box in place of the <u>underlined</u> word.

weep   delete   nearly   certain

1. Tara knew it was <u>almost</u> time to leave for school.

_____

_____

2. Ben began to <u>cry</u> when he could not find his dog.

_____

_____

3. Lily knew she should <u>erase</u> her last sentence.

_____

_____

4. David was <u>sure</u> he would win the race.

_____

_____

Fill in the bubble next to the correct answer.

1. Which word is a synonym for **nearly**?

   Ⓐ dearly

   Ⓑ always

   Ⓒ almost

   Ⓓ never

2. Which sentence contains a synonym for **delete**?

   Ⓐ I will write the word.

   Ⓑ I will erase the word.

   Ⓒ I will read the word.

   Ⓓ I will type the word.

3. Which sentence contains a synonym for **cry**?

   Ⓐ The little girl began to weep when her mother left.

   Ⓑ The little girl began to laugh when her mother left.

   Ⓒ The little girl began to yell when her mother left.

   Ⓓ The little girl began to talk when her mother left.

4. Which two words are synonyms?

   Ⓐ sure, unsure

   Ⓑ maybe, certain

   Ⓒ sure, possibly

   Ⓓ sure, certain

5. Which two words are synonyms?

   Ⓐ erase, invisible

   Ⓑ weep, wept

   Ⓒ nearly, almost

   Ⓓ almost, certain

Synonyms are words that have almost the same meaning.

Far is a synonym for **distant**.
Afraid is a synonym for **fearful**.

A. Write a synonym from the box for the underlined word in each sentence.

discover   vacant   fearful   distant

1. If the dark makes you feel underlined afraid, you are _____ .

2. A tree that is <u>far</u> away from you is _____ .

3. If you <u>find</u> a trail in the woods, you _____ it.

4. An <u>empty</u> house that no one lives in is _____ .

B. Circle the synonym for the bold word in each row.

1. **find**   lose   discover   search

2. **afraid**   fearful   brave   shy

3. **empty**   alone   full   vacant

4. **far**   away   distant   close

C. Circle the synonyms for **fearful** and **discover** in this sentence.

I was afraid I would not find my pencil before the spelling test!

Name: _____

Synonyms are words that have almost the same meaning.

Use a synonym from the box to write a sentence for each bold word. Underline the synonym.

distant   vacant   fearful   discover

1. Write a sentence using a synonym for **find**.

   _____

   _____

2. Write a sentence using a synonym for **empty**.

   _____

   _____

3. Write a sentence using a synonym for **far**.

   _____

   _____

4. Write a sentence using a synonym for **afraid**.

   _____

   _____

Synonyms are words that have almost the same meaning.

Fill in each blank with the best synonym from the box.

> afraid   find   far   empty
> fearful   discover   distant   vacant

Tim and his sister Julie wandered away from the campground.

Before long, they were lost. It was getting dark, and they both felt

_____. Julie looked around. Far away through the

trees, she could see a _____ cabin. When they got to

the cabin, Tim peeked through a window. There were no people inside.

The cabin was _____.

The door was not locked, so they went inside. Tim tried to

_____ something to eat, but there was no food. The

cabinets were all _____. Then Julie heard something

outside. Someone was calling her name! Tim and Julie ran outside to

_____ that their parents had found them.

"Thank goodness you are okay," said their mother. "We were so

_____ when you did not come back."

"You must not go so _____ from camp," said

their father. Tim and Julie knew he was right.

Synonyms are words that have almost the same meaning. A word may have more than one synonym.

Snooze and **rest** are synonyms for **nap**.
Chuckle and **giggle** are synonyms for **laugh**.

A. Complete each sentence with a synonym from the box.

> chuckle   reply   peek   rest

1. Another word for **answer** is _____ .

2. Another word for **nap** is _____ .

3. Another word for **look** is _____ .

4. Another word for **laugh** is _____ .

B. Complete each sentence with a synonym from the box.

> giggle   respond   peer   snooze

1. If you take a **nap**, you are having a _____ .

2. If you **answer** someone, you _____ to her.

3. When you **laugh** at a funny TV show, you _____ .

4. When you **look** at your friend, you _____ at him.

Name: _____

Synonyms are words that have almost the same meaning.

Choose a synonym from the box to replace the word under the line.

> rest   chuckle   reply   peer
>
> respond   snooze   peek   giggle

1. The little girl began to _____ at the clown.
   (laugh)

   The funny joke made Grandpa _____.
   (laugh)

2. Drew lay down to _____ after the big game.
   (sleep)

   Dad wanted to _____ on the couch.
   (sleep)

3. Karen wrote a _____ to the e-mail.
   (answer)

   Tom knew he had to _____ truthfully.
   (answer)

4. Cassie took a quick _____ at the birthday cake.
   (look)

   Mario wanted to _____ through the telescope.
   (look)

Name: _____

Fill in the bubble next to the correct answer.

1. Which word does <u>not</u> tell what a person would do after hearing a joke?

Ⓐ giggle
Ⓑ laugh
Ⓒ chuckle
Ⓓ sleep

2. Which word does <u>not</u> tell what a person would do if he were tired?

Ⓐ rest
Ⓑ shout
Ⓒ sleep
Ⓓ snooze

3. Which two words are synonyms for **answer**?

Ⓐ reply, ask
Ⓑ reply, speak
Ⓒ reply, respond
Ⓓ ask, respond

4. Which two words are synonyms for **look**?

Ⓐ peer, eye
Ⓑ peer, peek
Ⓒ know, peek
Ⓓ peer, peel

5. Which sentence contains synonyms for **answer** and **laugh**?

Ⓐ The teacher's reply made the class giggle.
Ⓑ The teacher's reply made the class cry.
Ⓒ The teacher's question made the class giggle.
Ⓓ The teacher's question made the class think.

Synonyms are words that have almost the same meaning. A word may have more than one synonym.

Repair and **mend** are synonyms for **fix**.
Toss and **pitch** are synonyms for **throw**.

A. Match each sentence to a synonym for the underlined word.

1. Can you gently throw the ball to me?   •   • repair

2. We need to fix our car before our trip.   •   • hurt

3. Be very careful not to harm the baby.   •   • piece

4. The model plane was missing a part.   •   • toss

B. Match each sentence to a synonym for the underlined word.

1. The puppy might harm the new carpet.   •   • section

2. The ending was the best part of the book.   •   • pitch

3. Can you please fix my broken doll?   •   • damage

4. I can throw the ball across the field!   •   • mend

C. Fill in each blank with an underlined word from above.

1. If you repair something, you _____ it.

2. When you toss a ball, you _____ it.

3. If you eat a piece of cake, you eat a _____ of the cake.

Synonyms are words that have almost the same meaning. A word may have more than one synonym.

A. Circle two synonyms for the bold word in each row.

1. **fix**   repair   try   mend   break

2. **throw**   catch   toss   pitch   hit

3. **part**   comb   cart   piece   section

4. **hurt**   harm   stop   have   damage

B. Use a synonym you circled above to write a sentence for each bold word. Underline the synonym.

1. Write a sentence using a synonym for **throw**.

   _____

   _____

2. Write a sentence using a synonym for **hurt**.

   _____

   _____

3. Write a sentence using a synonym for **part**.

   _____

   _____

Synonyms are words that have almost the same meaning.

Fill in each blank with the best synonym from the box.

fix	part	hurt	toss
repair	piece	damage	throw

This morning, my brother Greg tried to _____ a

ball to me while I was riding my bike. I tried to catch the ball, but I

crashed instead! It was scary, but I did not get _____.

When I picked up my bike, I saw that one of the tires was flat. I would

need help to _____ it.

I asked my dad to help me. He looked at my bike and said that the

tire would be easy to _____. He took my bike to the

_____ of the garage where he keeps the tools. He

showed me how to patch the tube inside the tire with a small

_____ of rubber. Soon, my bike was as good as new!

Then Dad had a talk with us. Dad told us that it is not safe to

_____ a ball at someone who is riding a bike. I could

have been hurt, and there could have been real _____

to the bike. We knew Dad was right. We won't do it again.

Synonyms are words that have almost the same meaning. A word may have more than one synonym.

Damp and **moist** are synonyms for **wet**.
Skinny, **slim**, and **slender** are synonyms for **thin**.

A. Circle the synonym for **strange** in each sentence.

1. Sophie thought her grandma's big red hat was odd.

2. It was unusual for Carl to skip dessert.

B. Circle the synonym for **wet** in each sentence.

1. My shirt was damp with sweat after the soccer game.

2. Dad said to get the sponge moist before wiping the table.

C. Circle the synonym for **surprised** in each sentence.

1. The magic show amazed everyone who saw it.

2. Jim was astonished to find a new bike in the driveway!

D. Circle the synonym for **skinny** in each sentence.

1. The lost puppy was thin and hungry when we found her.

2. The slender snake was wrapped around a branch.

3. The flower had a slim stem and sharp thorns!

Synonyms are words that have almost the same meaning. A word may have more than one synonym.

Use a synonym from the box to write a sentence for each bold word. Underline the synonym.

unusual   moist   astonished   thin

1. Write a sentence using a synonym for **wet**.

_____

_____

2. Write a sentence using a synonym for **skinny**.

_____

_____

3. Write a sentence using a synonym for **strange**.

_____

_____

4. Write a sentence using a synonym for **surprised**.

_____

_____

Fill in the bubble next to the correct answer.

1. Which word is <u>not</u> a synonym for **thin**?

   Ⓐ slender

   Ⓑ slim

   Ⓒ little

   Ⓓ skinny

2. Which two words are synonyms for **strange**?

   Ⓐ odd, unusual

   Ⓑ usual, unusual

   Ⓒ odd, normal

   Ⓓ odd, old

3. Which two words are synonyms for **wet**?

   Ⓐ damp, cold

   Ⓑ warm, dry

   Ⓒ moist, damp

   Ⓓ moist, dry

4. Which sentence contains synonyms for **amazed** and **odd**?

   Ⓐ We were surprised by her new hairstyle.

   Ⓑ We were upset by her unusual hairstyle.

   Ⓒ We were surprised by her adorable hairstyle.

   Ⓓ We were surprised by her unusual hairstyle.

5. Which sentence contains synonyms for **slender** and **damp**?

   Ⓐ My dog looks unusual when he is moist.

   Ⓑ My dog looks thin when he is tired.

   Ⓒ My dog looks skinny when he is wet.

   Ⓓ My dog looks odd when he is moist.

Use exact words to make your meaning clear.

words for *eat:* bite, chew, munch, gobble, nibble, chomp, dine
words for *drink:* sip, slurp, gulp, lap

A. Circle the word that makes the meaning clear.

eat   nibble

munch   eat

gobble   eat

eat   dine

B. Circle the word that makes the meaning clear.

drink   sip

lap   drink

drink   gulp

drink   slurp

Name: _____

Use exact words to make your meaning clear.

words for *eat:* bite, chew, munch, gobble, nibble, chomp, dine
words for *drink:* sip, slurp, gulp, lap

Complete each sentence with a word for **eat** or **drink**.
Choose the word from above that gives the clearest meaning.

1. You make a lot of noise if you _____ your soup.
   (drink)

2. Don't _____ carrot sticks during a movie!
   (eat)

3. My hamster likes to take his time and _____ his food.
   (eat)

4. When I _____ soda quickly, I feel sick.
   (drink)

5. On my birthday, the whole family will _____ at a restaurant.
   (eat)

6. The dog will _____ her bone and _____ water.
   (eat)   (drink)

7. My grandmother likes to chat with her friends while they _____ tea.
   (drink)

8. If you are hungry, _____ on an apple.
   (eat)

Use exact words to make your meaning clear.

words for *eat:* bite, chew, munch, gobble, nibble, chomp, dine
words for *drink:* sip, slurp, gulp, lap

Fill in each blank with a word for **eat** or **drink**.
Choose the word from above that gives the clearest meaning.

Grandpa Gus picked me up at 1:00 to go to the zoo. I was late, so

I had to _____ down my lunch. Grandpa brought bottles

of lemonade for us to _____ in the car. I still had a lot of

lemonade left when we parked the car, so I had to _____

it down.

We got to the zoo at feeding time. We found out that each animal

eats its food in its own way. Giraffes _____ on tiny leaves.

Lions _____ hungrily on meat and bones. Zebras

_____ on grass and hay.

Watching the animals eat made Grandpa and me hungry. We

were in luck! A sign at the zoo restaurant said, "Kids under 12

_____ free." I couldn't wait to _____

into a hot dog!

Use exact words to make your meaning clear.

words for *pretty:* glamorous, dazzling, handsome, adorable, good-looking, lovely, gorgeous, attractive

A. Circle the word that makes the meaning clear.

glamorous   adorable

lovely   handsome

lovely   glamorous

adorable   good-looking

B. Circle the word that makes the meaning clear.

adorable   attractive

gorgeous   handsome

dazzling   handsome

good-looking   glamorous

Use exact words to make your meaning clear.

words for *pretty*: glamorous, dazzling, handsome, adorable, good-looking, lovely, gorgeous, attractive

A. Complete each sentence with a word from the box.
   Choose the best word.

> attractive   adorable   gorgeous   good-looking

1. The playful kitten was _____ .

2. Tim bought a _____ suit to wear to the wedding.

3. The house was _____ to buyers because it had just been painted.

4. Susie wanted to buy the _____ red dress in the store window.

B. Complete each sentence with a word from the box.
   Choose the best word.

> lovely   dazzling   handsome   glamorous

1. Everyone was amazed by the _____ fireworks.

2. John's horse was a _____ black stallion.

3. Everyone said it was a _____ tea party.

4. The _____ hotel had a swimming pool with a waterfall.

Fill in the bubble next to the correct answer.

1. Which word best describes a puppy?

   Ⓐ dazzling

   Ⓑ good-looking

   Ⓒ adorable

   Ⓓ gorgeous

2. Which word best describes a bouquet of flowers?

   Ⓐ adorable

   Ⓑ lovely

   Ⓒ good-looking

   Ⓓ glamorous

3. Which word best describes a sparkling diamond necklace?

   Ⓐ handsome

   Ⓑ lovely

   Ⓒ dazzling

   Ⓓ adorable

4. Which word is not a good choice to describe a sunset?

   Ⓐ attractive

   Ⓑ dazzling

   Ⓒ lovely

   Ⓓ gorgeous

5. Which word is not a good choice to describe a jewel-covered gown?

   Ⓐ gorgeous

   Ⓑ adorable

   Ⓒ attractive

   Ⓓ glamorous

Use exact words to make your meaning clear.

words for *walk:* stroll, amble, march, hike, toddle
words for *run:* jog, race, dash, gallop, scamper

Circle the word that best describes the picture.

walk   march   toddle   walk

hike   walk   walk   stroll

run   gallop   race   run

dash   run   run   scamper

Use exact words to make your meaning clear.

words for *walk:* stroll, amble, march, hike, toddle
words for *run:* jog, race, dash, gallop, scamper

Complete each sentence with a word for **walk** or **run**.
Choose the word from above that gives the clearest meaning.

1. I like to _____ in the woods.
    (walk)

2. My brother and I always _____ home from school.
    (run)

3. I need to _____ to the store for some milk.
    (run)

4. If we _____ slowly to the park, it will take an hour.
    (walk)

5. I watched the baby _____ to his mother.
    (walk)

6. Sarah made her horse _____ across the field.
    (run)

7. The family likes to _____ around the block after dinner.
    (walk)

8. Mom tries to _____ two miles every day.
    (run)

Fill in the bubble next to the correct answer.

1. Which word is <u>not</u> another word for **run**?

Ⓐ dash

Ⓑ race

Ⓒ stroll

Ⓓ scamper

2. Which word is <u>not</u> another word for **walk**?

Ⓐ jog

Ⓑ stroll

Ⓒ hike

Ⓓ toddle

3. Which word best describes how a mouse would **run**?

Ⓐ amble

Ⓑ scamper

Ⓒ jog

Ⓓ gallop

4. Which word best describes how a group of soldiers would **walk**?

Ⓐ march

Ⓑ amble

Ⓒ stroll

Ⓓ toddle

5. Which sentence uses the best word for **walk**?

Ⓐ Today, we will hike five miles to our campsite.

Ⓑ Today, we will stroll five miles to our campsite.

Ⓒ Today, we will toddle five miles to our campsite.

Ⓓ Today, we will amble five miles to our campsite.

Use exact words to make your meaning clear.

words for *little*: teeny, petite, miniature, wee, minute, undersized

A. Circle the word that makes the meaning clear.

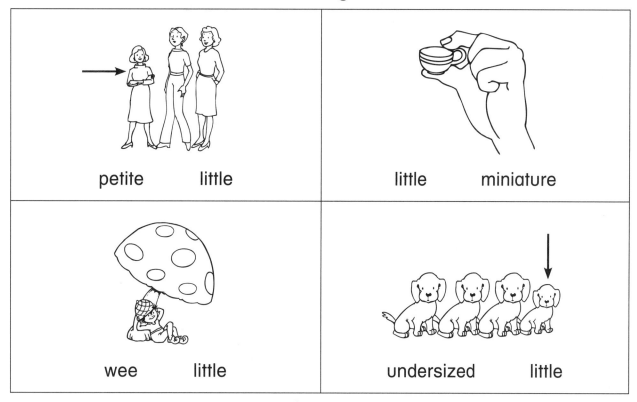

petite little	little miniature
wee little	undersized little

B. Complete each sentence with a word for **little**.
   Use the words at the top of the page.

1. Allison could hold the _____ kitten in one hand.

2. The dollhouse was full of _____ furniture.

3. The _____ fairy sat on a flower petal.

4. The _____ shirt will not fit Seth.

Use exact words to make your meaning clear.

words for *big*: enormous, huge, gigantic, immense, massive

Use a different word for **big** to write each sentence.

1. Write a sentence about an elephant, using the word **enormous**.

_____

_____

2. Write a sentence about the ocean, using the word **immense**.

_____

_____

3. Write a sentence about an ice-cream sundae, using the word **gigantic**.

_____

_____

4. Write a sentence about a dinosaur, using the word **huge**.

_____

_____

5. Write a sentence about a building, using the word **massive**.

_____

_____

Name: _____

Use exact words to make your meaning clear.

Fill in each blank with the best word from the box.
You will <u>not</u> use one of the words.

teeny	huge	gigantic	minute
immense	petite	miniature	enormous

Allen was going to fly in an airplane for the first time! He was going

with his mom to visit his grandma in New York. Allen was looking forward

to visiting such a _____ city. Allen's bag was not too

big, but his mother's suitcase was _____. Allen's mom

was a _____ woman, so it was a good thing that her

suitcase had wheels!

Allen was lucky to get a seat by the window. Taking off was exciting!

As they went higher, the buildings below looked _____.

The cars looked like _____ toy cars. But soon, they

were flying over mountains. Even from high up in the sky, Allen could tell

that the mountains were _____.

The flight attendant came by. She gave them each

a cup of water and a _____ bag

of pretzels. Soon, it was time to land. Allen hoped

they would eat dinner right away. He was still hungry!

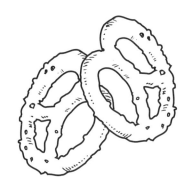

Use exact words to make your meaning clear.
Said is not a very exact word. Things can be said
in different ways.

> **quiet words for** *said:* whispered, murmured
> **loud words for** *said:* shouted, yelled, exclaimed

A. Read each sentence. Is it quiet or loud?
Choose the best word from under the line to make the meaning clear.

1. Hannah _____ a secret to her friend.
   (whispered, shouted)

2. The lost girl _____ for her mother.
   (shouted, murmured)

3. The crowd _____ when the home team scored.
   (whispered, yelled)

4. "You stole my bike!" the boy _____ angrily.
   (murmured, exclaimed)

5. Tim softly _____ that he was sorry.
   (exclaimed, murmured)

B. Match each statement to the word that best describes
how it was said.

1. "Help, I can't swim! Help!" •   • exclaimed

2. "Please don't wake the baby." •   • shouted

3. "I don't want to take a bath!" •   • whispered

Name: _____

Precise Language

Unit 5

Use exact words to make your meaning clear.
Said is not a very exact word. Things can be said
in different ways.

words for *said*: declared, stated, mentioned, remarked, answered,
replied, announced, uttered

A. Complete each sentence with the best word from the box.

> replied   declared   mentioned   announced

1. "There will be a fire drill today," the principal _____.

2. "You're welcome," Laura _____ to her friend.

3. "I already did my homework," Andrew _____ proudly.

4. "You have a stain on your shirt," Jenny _____ to her sister.

B. Complete each sentence with the best word from the box.

> stated   remarked   answered   uttered

1. "A noun is a person, place, or thing," the teacher _____.

2. "I'm over here!" Danny _____ when he heard his
   mother call.

3. The parents were so excited when their baby _____ his
   first word.

4. "The bride looks lovely," Aunt Clara _____ to Uncle Ned.

Fill in the bubble next to the correct answer.

1. Which word is <u>not</u> another word for **said**?

   Ⓐ stated

   Ⓑ mentioned

   Ⓒ smiled

   Ⓓ declared

2. Which word would you use for someone who said something quietly?

   Ⓐ remarked

   Ⓑ murmured

   Ⓒ exclaimed

   Ⓓ shouted

3. Which two words would you use if someone said something loudly?

   Ⓐ whispered, shouted

   Ⓑ answered, yelled

   Ⓒ yelled, declared

   Ⓓ shouted, yelled

4. Which word for **said** would best complete the following sentence?
   "By the way, I saw the Browns' new puppy today," Mom _____ .

   Ⓐ mentioned

   Ⓑ shouted

   Ⓒ whispered

   Ⓓ murmured

5. Which sentence uses the best <u>underlined</u> word for **said**?

   Ⓐ "It's nice to meet you, too," Kim <u>whispered</u> to her new teacher.

   Ⓑ "It's nice to meet you, too," Kim <u>uttered</u> to her new teacher.

   Ⓒ "It's nice to meet you, too," Kim <u>announced</u> to her new teacher.

   Ⓓ "It's nice to meet you, too," Kim <u>replied</u> to her new teacher.

Use exact words to make your meaning clear.
Nice is not a very exact word. Weather can be nice.
A person can be nice. You can have a nice time.

nice **weather:** pleasant, fabulous, favorable, magnificent
nice **person:** friendly, caring, charming, kind
nice **time:** fun-filled, enjoyable, amusing, entertaining

A. Circle the best word to replace **nice** in each sentence.

1. What **nice** weather we are having!   magnificent   caring

2. Sasha is always **nice** to animals.   entertaining   kind

3. We had a **nice** time at camp.   charming   fun-filled

4. The weather is **nice** in springtime.   pleasant   amusing

B. Read each sentence.
Is it about the weather, a person, or a time?
Choose the best word from the top of the page to fill in
each blank.

1. The _____ teacher made all the students happy.

2. We had an _____ time at the circus today.

3. The weather is _____ for a picnic.

4. Cody had an _____ time at the party.

5. You won't need an umbrella. The weather is _____ today.

6. The _____ police officer gave us directions to the park.

Name: _____

Use exact words to make your meaning clear.
Nice is not a very exact word. Weather can be nice.
A person can be nice. You can have a nice time.

nice weather: pleasant, fabulous, favorable, magnificent
nice person: friendly, caring, charming, kind
nice time: fun-filled, enjoyable, amusing, entertaining

Rewrite each sentence, using a word from above to replace
the word **nice**.

1. The weather was **nice** for the outdoor party.

   _____

   _____

2. It was **nice** of Ashley to bring the desserts.

   _____

   _____

3. Tom and Steve had a **nice** time at the party.

   _____

   _____

4. The **nice** party host thanked everyone for coming.

   _____

   _____

5. All of the guests thought the party was **nice**.

   _____

   _____

Name: _____

Use exact words to make your meaning clear.

nice weather: pleasant, fabulous, favorable, magnificent
nice person: friendly, caring, charming, kind
nice time: fun-filled, enjoyable, amusing, entertaining

Fill in each blank with the best word from above.
Use a word only once.

The sun was shining and the weather was _____!

Ethan's family decided to go to the fair. First, they went to see the animals.

There were cows, pigs, horses, and rabbits. A _____ girl

let Ethan hold her rabbit. It was warm and soft.

On the way to get some lunch, Ethan got lost! Luckily, a

_____ woman helped him find his family. After lunch, they

had an _____ time watching a funny clown. Then, Ethan

and his mom had a _____ time riding the roller coaster!

It was getting late. They thought about going home, but the weather

was still _____, so they stayed a bit longer. While they

were eating ice cream, a _____ man in a sweater gave

Ethan a balloon. Finally, it was time to go home. What an

_____ time at the fair!

Antonyms are words that have opposite meanings.

Heavy is an antonym for **light**.
Backward is an antonym for **forward**.

Circle the antonym that matches the picture.

neat   sloppy

dull   shiny

light   heavy

tame   wild

wild   tame

heavy   light

forward   backward

sloppy   neat

Antonyms are words that have opposite meanings.

A. Draw lines to match the <u>underlined</u> word in each sentence to its antonym.

1. Jim carried his <u>light</u> backpack.   •   • shiny

2. The paint looked <u>dull</u> after it dried. •   • wild

3. Jean can only skate <u>forward</u>.   •   • neat

4. Britney has <u>sloppy</u> handwriting.   •   • heavy

5. The bear cub at the zoo was <u>tame</u>. •   • backward

B. Follow the directions. Use antonyms from above.

1. Write a sentence using an antonym for **light**.

_____

_____

2. Write a sentence using an antonym for **neat**.

_____

_____

3. Write a sentence using an antonym for **tame**.

_____

_____

Fill in the bubble next to the correct answer.

1. Antonyms are words that _____ .

Ⓐ have opposite meanings

Ⓑ have nearly the same meaning

Ⓒ sound the same but have different meanings

Ⓓ are made from two smaller words

2. Which word is an antonym for **wild**?

Ⓐ child

Ⓑ animal

Ⓒ kitten

Ⓓ tame

3. Which two words are antonyms?

Ⓐ shiny, tiny

Ⓑ rough, dull

Ⓒ dull, shiny

Ⓓ shiny, slippery

4. Which two words are antonyms?

Ⓐ heavy, weight

Ⓑ feather, light

Ⓒ light, heavy

Ⓓ bright, light

5. Which sentence contains an antonym for **sloppy**?

Ⓐ Jenna's room was small.

Ⓑ Jenna's room was messy.

Ⓒ Jenna's room was empty.

Ⓓ Jenna's room was neat.

Antonyms are words that have opposite meanings.

Above is an antonym for **below**.
Sharp is an antonym for **dull.**

A. Choose an antonym from the box to replace each word under the line.

rough   least   together   dull   above

1. The boys played _____ at the playground.
   (apart)

2. We rode our bikes on the _____ road.
   (smooth)

3. Paul's pencil tip was _____.
   (sharp)

4. Jean keeps the plates _____ the bowls.
   (below)

5. Kayla earned the _____ amount of money.
   (most)

B. Fill in each blank with one of the words from the box.

1. **Apart** is an antonym for _____.

2. **Most** is an antonym for _____.

3. **Smooth** is an antonym for _____.

Name: _____

Antonyms are words that have opposite meanings.

A. Circle the antonym for the bold word in each row.

1. **apart**   piece   above   together

2. **least**   most   more   less

3. **rough**   hard   smooth   shiny

4. **above**   below   over   around

5. **dull**   soft   afraid   sharp

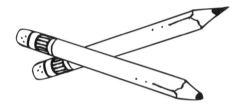

B. Write sentences. Use a word you circled above in each sentence.

1. _____

_____

2. _____

_____

3. _____

_____

4. _____

_____

5. _____

_____

Antonyms are words that have opposite meanings.

Fill in each blank with the best antonym from the box.

rough   apart   least   above

smooth   together   most   below

Jake and Cal are best friends. They spend _____

of their time with each other. Yesterday, Jake and Cal went fishing

_____.

When they got to the lake, the water was still and as

_____ as glass. They sat on the dock to fish. They

sat _____ from each other so their fishing lines

would not get tangled. They could see fish swimming in the water

_____ them. Soon, Jake had a bite! He reeled in his

line until the fish was on the dock. The fish was silver with thick,

_____ scales.

After a while, Cal looked at the sky _____ them.

He saw big, gray storm clouds. It was time to go home. This was

the _____ amount of fish they had ever caught,

but they still had a great time together.

Antonyms are words that have opposite meanings.

Few is an antonym for **many**.
Always is an antonym for **never**.

A. Read each pair of sentences.
   Circle the word that is an antonym for the <u>underlined</u> word.

   1. Dad's car is <u>wide</u>. It was hard to drive it up the narrow driveway.

   2. Andy wanted to <u>sell</u> his baseball cards. Derek wanted to buy them.

   3. The forecaster said the rain would <u>increase</u> in the morning.
      Perhaps it will decrease by the afternoon.

   4. Jody made many cookies. She gave her sister only a <u>few</u> of them.

   5. Sharon always wore her boots when it rained. Her feet <u>never</u> got wet.

B. Use one of the <u>underlined</u> words above to complete
   each sentence.

   1. **Buy** is an antonym for _____ .

   2. **Many** is an antonym for _____ .

   3. **Narrow** is an antonym for _____ .

   4. **Decrease** is an antonym for _____ .

   5. **Always** is an antonym for _____ .

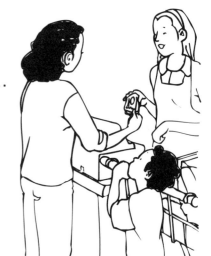

Antonyms are words that have opposite meanings.

A. Read each sentence.
   Use an antonym from the box to write a sentence
   that has the opposite meaning.

> never   many   narrow   buy   decrease

1. Carly wanted to <u>sell</u> cookies at the fair.

   _____

2. Ben ate too <u>few</u> pancakes.

   _____

3. Kenny <u>always</u> combs his hair before school.

   _____

4. The store plans to <u>increase</u> its prices.

   _____

5. Susie walked down the <u>wide</u> hallway.

   _____

B. Circle the antonym for the bold word in each row.

   1. **decrease**   less   few   increase

   2. **many**   few   more   some

   3. **narrow**   thin   wide   fat

Name: _____

Fill in the bubble next to the correct answer.

1. Which word is an antonym for **increase**?

   Ⓐ decrease

   Ⓑ add

   Ⓒ into

   Ⓓ delight

2. Which sentence contains an antonym for **few**?

   Ⓐ John has more pennies.

   Ⓑ John has two pennies.

   Ⓒ John has many pennies.

   Ⓓ John has less pennies.

3. Which sentence contains an antonym for **never**?

   Ⓐ Chris rarely wears a hat.

   Ⓑ Chris always wears a hat.

   Ⓒ Chris usually wears a hat.

   Ⓓ Chris sometimes wears a hat.

4. Which two words are antonyms?

   Ⓐ buy, spend

   Ⓑ cell, sell

   Ⓒ buy, sell

   Ⓓ buy, store

5. Which two words are antonyms?

   Ⓐ narrow, skinny

   Ⓑ narrow, large

   Ⓒ across, wide

   Ⓓ narrow, wide

Antonyms are words that have opposite meanings.

Spend is an antonym for **save**.
Odd is an antonym for **even**.

A. Fill in the blank with the correct antonym.

1. Twenty-four is an _____ number.
   (odd, even)

2. Jim's shoes were so _____ that they fell off his feet.
   (loose, tight)

3. Riding a bike without a helmet is a _____ choice.
   (wise, foolish)

4. The _____ water felt good on the hot afternoon.
   (warm, cool)

5. Pedro wanted to _____ his money at the store.
   (spend, save)

B. Circle the antonyms in each sentence.

1. Mandy's shirt was loose, but her sandals were tight.

2. The foolish girl did not follow her friend's wise advice.

3. Jacob had to save his money for a long time before he could spend it on a bike.

4. We will solve the math problems with odd numbers and skip the problems with even numbers.

Antonyms are words that have opposite meanings.

A. Read each sentence.
   Use an antonym from the box to write a sentence
   that has the opposite meaning.

> warm   foolish   tight   spend

1. Tom wanted to <u>save</u> his money.

   _____

2. There was a <u>cool</u> breeze at the beach.

   _____

3. Tad gave his little brother <u>wise</u> advice.

   _____

4. Dad made a <u>loose</u> knot in the rope.

   _____

B. Use one of the <u>underlined</u> words above to complete
   each sentence.

1. **Warm** is an antonym for _____ .

2. **Tight** is an antonym for _____ .

3. **Spend** is an antonym for _____ .

4. **Foolish** is an antonym for _____ .

Antonyms are words that have opposite meanings.

Fill in each blank with the best antonym from the box.

wise	tight	save	cool
foolish	loose	spend	warm

"Let's go to the beach!" exclaimed Dad. At first, Mom thought it was

a _____ idea because there were a lot of chores to do

at home. Dad said that the weather was too _____

to do chores. Mom had to agree.

Lisa put on her swimsuit. She had grown since last summer and it

was too _____! Luckily, her big sister Ann found one she

had outgrown. Ann's old swimsuit was a little _____

on Lisa, but she could wear it.

At the beach, the girls went swimming in the _____

water. Then Mom gave them each some money to _____

on ice cream. Lisa wanted to _____ her money, but

the ice cream looked too good not to eat!

After ice cream, Mom said it would be _____ to wait

a few minutes before going back into the water. The girls built a sand castle

while waiting. Then they took one more swim before going home.

Antonyms are words that have opposite meanings.

Depart is an antonym for **arrive**.
North is an antonym for **south**.

A. Replace each <u>underlined</u> word with an antonym from the box.

> badly   depart   polite   south   host

1. Jared was a <u>guest</u> at the party.   _____

2. Tammy was <u>rude</u> to her aunt.   _____

3. Ethan watched the plane <u>arrive</u>.   _____

4. Carlos did <u>well</u> on the test.   _____

5. The park was <u>north</u> of the school.   _____

B. Draw lines to match the antonyms.

1. polite   •   • arrive

2. host   •   • north

3. depart   •   • well

4. badly   •   • rude

5. south   •   • guest

C. Circle the two antonyms in each sentence.

1. A good host makes every guest feel welcome.

2. Kim was polite at the dinner table, but her sister was rude.

Antonyms are words that have opposite meanings.

A. Circle the antonym for the bold word in each row.

1. **polite**   kind   rude   please

2. **south**   north   map   east

3. **guest**   party   friend   host

4. **arrive**   depart   land   enter

5. **well**   good   badly   nice

B. Write sentences.
Underline the antonym in each sentence.

1. Write a sentence using an antonym for **polite**.

_____

_____

2. Write a sentence using an antonym for **well**.

_____

_____

3. Write a sentence using an antonym for **host**.

_____

_____

Antonyms are words that have opposite meanings.

Fill in each blank with an antonym from the box.

host	rude	arrive	well
guest	polite	depart	badly

It was almost time for Sasha's birthday party! She could not wait

for her friends to _____. Sasha heard a knock. Her

first _____ was at the door! Sasha let her friend in.

Soon, all her friends were there.

Sasha wanted to be a good _____. She did not

get upset when she did _____ in a game. When her

friend Kim did _____, Sasha said, "Good job!"

Then, it was time to open presents. Sasha remembered to be

_____ and say "thank you" for each gift. Next, it was

time for cake and ice cream. Sasha tried not to chew with her mouth

open. She did not want to be _____ at her own

birthday party!

When it was time for her guests to _____,

Sasha made sure to thank each one for coming. It had been

her best birthday party yet!

 Vocabulary Fundamentals • EMC 2802 • © Evan-Moor Corp.

Homophones are words that sound alike.
They have different spellings and different meanings.

pear: "a fruit"
pair: "two things that go together"

Circle the correct homophone.

flour flower	meat meet
sun son	hair hare
meet meat	son sun
hare hair	flower flour

Name: _____

Homophones are words that sound alike.
They have different spellings and different meanings.

A. Write the correct homophone on the line.

1. The _____ was hidden by the clouds.
   (son, sun)

2. I always braid my _____ before school.
   (hair, hare)

3. Can you _____ me at the park later?
   (meat, meet)

4. Emily picked a yellow _____ for her mother.
   (flower, flour)

5. Jim likes a lot of _____ on his sandwich.
   (meet, meat)

6. Mr. Jones took his _____ camping last week.
   (son, sun)

7. Perry needed two cups of _____ for the cake.
   (flour, flower)

8. Carla saw a wild _____ in the woods.
   (hair, hare)

B. Draw pictures to show a homophone pair from above.
   Write the correct homophone under each picture.

_____	_____

   Vocabulary Fundamentals • EMC 2802 • © Evan-Moor Corp.

Fill in the bubble next to the correct answer.

1. Homophones are words that _____.

   Ⓐ have opposite meanings

   Ⓑ have nearly the same meaning

   Ⓒ sound alike but have different spellings and meanings

   Ⓓ are made from two smaller words

2. Which two words are homophones?

   Ⓐ sun, son

   Ⓑ sun, star

   Ⓒ sun, moon

   Ⓓ son, boy

3. Which sentence is written correctly?

   Ⓐ I can meat you at 6:00 tonight.

   Ⓑ Kevin does not eat meet.

   Ⓒ I am going to meet my aunt at the airport.

   Ⓓ Let's meat for lunch next week.

4. Which sentence is written correctly?

   Ⓐ Look at that pretty pink flour.

   Ⓑ Chris added the flour while Jill stirred.

   Ⓒ I need three cups of flower for the cookies.

   Ⓓ Mark picked a white flour for his mother.

5. Which sentence is written correctly?

   Ⓐ I have curly hare.

   Ⓑ Tony has short hare.

   Ⓒ We saw a hair jump behind a tree.

   Ⓓ Sharon has long hair.

Name: _____

Homophones are words that sound alike.
They have different spellings and different meanings.

        see: "to look"
        sea: "an ocean"

A. Circle the correct homophone.

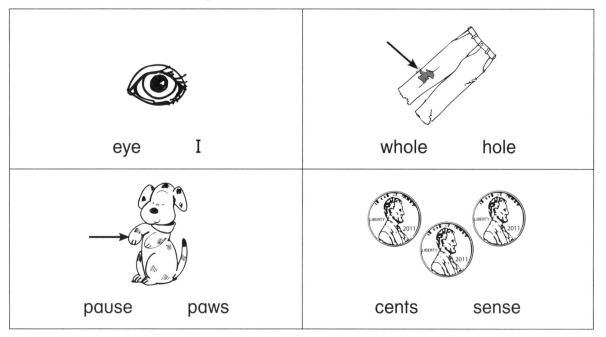

eye I	whole hole
pause paws	cents sense

B. Circle the correct homophone for each clue.

1. to stop for a moment   pause   paws

2. another word for **me**   eye   I

3. something that is <u>not</u> split into parts   whole   hole

4. hearing or smelling   cents   sense

C. Fill in the blanks with a pair of homophones from above.

_____ got sand in my _____ at the beach.

Name: _____

Homophones are words that sound alike.
They have different spellings and different meanings.

A. Cross out the incorrect homophone in each sentence.
Rewrite the sentence correctly, using a homophone
from the box.

> hole   I   paws   cents

1. The puppy has brown and white pause.

    _____

2. I have fifty sense in my pocket.

    _____

3. Today, eye went to the park with my brother.

    _____

    _____

4. There is a big whole in my shirt.

    _____

B. Complete each sentence with a homophone pair from above.

1. The _____ class helped dig a _____ to
   plant a tree.

2. It made good _____ to spend fifty _____ on
   a bottle of water.

Homophones are words that sound alike.
They have different spellings and different meanings.

Fill in each blank with the best homophone from the box.

eye	I	paws	sense
cents	hole	pause	whole

Today, I played hide-and-seek with my friends. I got to count first.

When _____ opened my eyes, everyone was gone. I

stood very still. I heard a noise. I could _____ that

someone was nearby. I looked behind the door. There was Tom!

Then, I looked in my bedroom. I peeked in the clothes hamper.

There was Brett! He had gotten his _____ body inside!

After that, I looked under the bed. I did not find any of my friends, but I

did find fourteen _____ .

I wondered where to search next. I decided to _____

for a moment to think. Then I saw something move out of the corner of

my _____ . It was my dog, Skip. Skip is brown and white with

black _____ . Skip started to bark. He ran out of the bedroom.

I ran after him. He ran right to my playhouse in the corner of the family

room. I peeked through a _____ in the side. There was

Amelia! I had found everyone!

Name: _____

Homophones are words that sound alike.
They have different spellings and different meanings.

its: "belongs to it" **it's:** "it is"

two: "the number **2**" **too:** "also" **to:** "toward"

A. Complete each sentence with **its** or **it's**.

1. _____ almost time for dinner.

2. The cat licked _____ paws.

3. Do you think _____ going to snow today?

4. The jacket is missing one of _____ buttons.

5. I know _____ going to be a great party!

B. Complete each sentence with **two**, **too**, or **to**.

1. I want to go to the park, _____.

2. Please give the ball _____ Matt.

3. John ate _____ scoops of ice cream.

4. Pedro went _____ the store with his brother.

5. I checked out _____ books from the library.

6. My friend checked out books, _____.

7. It took us only _____ minutes to walk

   _____ school.

Homophones are words that sound alike.
They have different spellings and different meanings.

its: "belongs to it"   **it's:** "it is"

two: "the number 2"   **too:** "also"   **to:** "toward"

A. Cross out the incorrect homophone in each sentence.
   Write the correct homophone on the line.

   1. I would like a cookie, to.   _____

   2. We have too kittens.   _____

   3. Can we go two Grandma's house now?   _____

   4. I know how to ride a bike, two.   _____

   5. Marla did all her chores, to.   _____

   6. I brought too pencils to school.   _____

B. Write a sentence using each homophone.
   Underline the homophone.

   1. **its:** _____

   _____

   2. **it's:** _____

   _____

Fill in the bubble next to the correct answer.

1. Which sentence is written correctly?

   Ⓐ Katie walked two the popcorn stand.

   Ⓑ Katie bought to bags of popcorn.

   Ⓒ Cindy ate some popcorn, too.

   Ⓓ Cindy wanted some soda, two.

2. Which sentence is written correctly?

   Ⓐ It's my birthday today!

   Ⓑ Its a great day for a party.

   Ⓒ One of the balloons is missing it's string.

   Ⓓ Mom says its time to open presents!

3. Which sentence is written correctly?

   Ⓐ Greg and Mario walked too the park.

   Ⓑ Mario went down the slide two times.

   Ⓒ Greg went down the slide, to.

   Ⓓ Greg and Mario stayed at the park for about too hours.

4. Which sentence is not written correctly?

   Ⓐ It's fun to draw animals.

   Ⓑ Yesterday, I drew a cat licking its paws.

   Ⓒ I had a hard time drawing it's ears.

   Ⓓ I think it's a good picture.

5. Which sentence is not written correctly?

   Ⓐ Can we go to the ice-cream shop?

   Ⓑ Mom says we can go in two minutes.

   Ⓒ I want hot fudge and whipped cream, to.

   Ⓓ Mom got two scoops of chocolate ice cream.

Homophones are words that sound alike.
They have different spellings and different meanings.

tail: "part of an animal"
tale: "a story"

A. Write the correct homophone on each line.

heard   herd

1. I saw a _____ of cows on the farm.

   This morning, I _____ them mooing.

know   no

2. I _____ where the cookies are kept.

   But there are _____ cookies left.

dear   deer

3. I saw a _____ in the woods.

   Oh _____, I forgot the camera!

wear   where

4. I want to _____ my red shirt today.

   I wonder _____ my red shirt is.

B. Complete each sentence with the correct pair of homophones
from above.

1. I don't _____ why there are _____ pencils left.

2. I don't know _____ I left the shoes I want to _____.

Homophones are words that sound alike.
They have different spellings and different meanings.

A. Write a sentence using each homophone.
Underline the homophone in each sentence.

1. **no:** _____

_____

2. **know:** _____

_____

3. **herd:** _____

_____

4. **heard:** _____

_____

5. **dear:** _____

_____

6. **deer:** _____

_____

B. Write a sentence using the homophones **where** and **wear**.
Underline the homophones in the sentence.

_____

_____

Homophones are words that sound alike.
They have different spellings and different meanings.

Fill in each blank with the correct homophone from the box.

dear	herd	no	wear
deer	heard	know	where

Today, I went for a hike in the woods with my dad. It was a warm day,

so I decided to _____ a T-shirt and shorts. We left early.

There were _____ sounds in the house because everyone

was asleep. We drove for a long time. I wondered _____ we

were going. Finally, we got to the trailhead.

Dad and I hiked up the trail for a while. Then we _____

a noise from the bushes. There were a mother _____ and her

fawn! We stood very still. Then some noisy people came up behind us.

The deer and her fawn ran away. I was upset, but Dad said it was not

their fault. They did not _____ the deer were there.

Soon, we came to a large meadow. We found a place near a stream

to eat lunch.

"Oh _____," said Dad. "I forgot the apples."

I did not mind. After lunch, we saw a whole _____ of deer

across the meadow. It was a great hike!

Homophones are words that sound alike.
They have different spellings and different meanings.

> **ant:** "an insect"
> **aunt:** "a relative"

A. Circle the correct homophone.

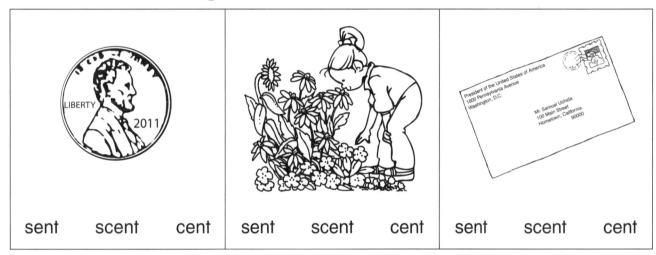

sent scent cent	sent scent cent	sent scent cent

B. Circle the correct homophone. Write it on the line.

1. If you drop a lamp, it will _____.   (brake, break)

2. When you stop a car, you _____.   (brake, break)

3. If you eat part of a pie, you eat _____ of it.   (sum, some)

4. When you add two numbers, you get a _____.   (sum, some)

5. The opposite of **war** is _____.   (piece, peace)

6. You need every _____ of a puzzle.   (piece, peace)

7. If you have a penny, you have one _____.   (cent, sent)

8. Perfume has a strong _____.   (scent, sent)

Name: _____

Homophones are words that sound alike.
They have different spellings and different meanings.

A. Complete each sentence with the correct homophone
   from the box.

> piece   sum   sent   scent
> peace   some   cent

1. I added the numbers to get the correct _____.

2. Tara had a _____ of chocolate cake.

3. My grandma _____ me a birthday gift.

4. Mom said she just wanted five minutes of _____.

5. The garden was filled with the _____ of roses.

6. I brought _____ cookies to school to share.

7. You cannot buy much if you only have one _____.

B. Write a sentence using each homophone.
   Underline the homophone.

1. **break:** _____

   _____

2. **brake:** _____

   _____

Fill in the bubble next to the correct answer.

1. Which two words are homophones?

   Ⓐ peace, war

   Ⓑ piece, peace

   Ⓒ piece, part

   Ⓓ peace, please

2. Which sentence is written correctly?

   Ⓐ I did sum of my math homework this morning.

   Ⓑ I had to add sum numbers together.

   Ⓒ Some of the problems were easy.

   Ⓓ I added 6 plus 4 and got a some of 10.

3. Which sentence is written correctly?

   Ⓐ David did not mean to break the radio.

   Ⓑ You could get a ticket if you brake the speed limit.

   Ⓒ A good driver will break at every red light.

   Ⓓ Kim thought the rock would brake her windshield.

4. Which sentence is written correctly?

   Ⓐ Dad cent flowers to Mom at work.

   Ⓑ Dad scent a card along with the flowers.

   Ⓒ The sent of the flowers filled the whole office.

   Ⓓ Mom sent Dad an e-mail to thank him for the flowers.

5. Which sentence is written correctly?

   Ⓐ I had to brake the cookie to give a piece to my friend.

   Ⓑ I had to break the cookie to give a peace to my friend.

   Ⓒ I had to brake the cookie to give a peace to my friend.

   Ⓓ I had to break the cookie to give a piece to my friend.

Name: _____

Homophones are words that sound alike.
They have different spellings and different meanings.

> **right:** "correct"
> **write:** "to make words with a pencil"

A. Write the correct homophone on each line.

1. Tony walked down the _____ to his classroom.
   (hall, haul)

   Maria had to _____ the heavy books home.
   (hall, haul)

2. Tom went outside to chop some _____ for the fire.
   (wood, would)

   Lucy knew it _____ be a great day.
   (wood, would)

3. Nathan wore his _____ shirt to the party.
   (red, read)

   Danny _____ a book on the bus.
   (red, read)

B. Write a sentence using the homophones **would** and **wood**.

_____

_____

Vocabulary Fundamentals • EMC 2802 • © Evan-Moor Corp.

Homophones are words that sound alike.
They have different spellings and different meanings.

> **their:** "belonging to them"
> **they're:** "they are"
> **there:** "a location or place"

A. Write **their**, **they're**, or **there** on each line.

1. I can see them over _____ .

2. The children left _____ coats inside.

3. _____ all going to the movies tonight.

4. Ben and Mary like sprinkles on _____ ice cream.

5. We will be able to see the parade if we stand over _____ .

6. I think _____ all ready now.

B. Cross out the incorrect homophones in each sentence.
Rewrite the sentence correctly.

1. There all waiting over their.

_____

_____

2. Their putting there shoes on over they're.

_____

_____

Homophones are words that sound alike.
They have different spellings and different meanings.

Fill in each blank with the best homophone from the box.

wood	hall	red	their	there
would	haul	read	they're	

Tim and Mark needed a bookshelf for _____ room.

Dad went to the store and came home with a big box.

"Where is the bookshelf?" asked Tim.

"It is in _____," replied Dad, pointing to the box.

"We have to put it together. _____ you two like to help?"

First, Tim and Mark helped their dad _____ the box

to the garage. Next, Dad _____ the instructions carefully.

Then, they got to work. Tim and Mark helped to hammer in the nails.

When it was done, they sanded the _____ to make it

smooth. Then, they painted the shelf bright _____.

After the paint dried, they carried the bookshelf down the

_____ to Tim and Mark's room. It looked great!

"Where are all your books?" asked Dad.

"_____ in the closet," said Mark. "Now we can put

them on our new bookshelf!"

 Vocabulary Fundamentals • EMC 2802 • © Evan-Moor Corp.

Homographs are words that are spelled the same but have different meanings.

A **duck** can be a kind of bird.
You might **duck** to avoid being hit by something.

Read each pair of sentences.
Match each sentence to the correct picture.

Drew watched the airplane <u>land</u>.

The <u>land</u> was dry and sandy.

The goose has an orange <u>bill</u>.

Mom paid the phone <u>bill</u>.

We have a swing set in our <u>yard</u>.

There are 3 feet in a <u>yard</u>.

Tyler saw a <u>duck</u> at the pond.

Ryan had to <u>duck</u> under a branch.

Homographs are words that are spelled the same but have different meanings.

A. Read the two meanings for the <u>underlined</u> word.
   Circle the meaning used in the sentence.

1. Jim's dad had to <u>duck</u> to get through the playhouse doorway.
   - to bend down to avoid hitting something
   - a kind of bird with webbed feet

2. The sailor saw <u>land</u> ahead.
   - to touch the ground
   - part of the Earth not covered by water

3. The waiter brought the <u>bill</u> to the table.
   - the beak of certain birds
   - a piece of paper showing how much money a person owes

4. Our <u>yard</u> has three trees and a lot of bushes.
   - a grassy area near a house
   - a unit of measure

B. Write your own sentences for each meaning of **duck**.

1. "to bend down quickly":

   _____

   _____

2. "a kind of bird":

   _____

   _____

Fill in the bubble next to the correct answer.

1. Which word has more than one meaning?

   Ⓐ owl

   Ⓑ duck

   Ⓒ rabbit

   Ⓓ lion

2. Which word does <u>not</u> have more than one meaning?

   Ⓐ yard

   Ⓑ bill

   Ⓒ car

   Ⓓ land

3. Which one is <u>not</u> a meaning of the word **land**?

   Ⓐ "a baby sheep"

   Ⓑ "to arrive by airplane"

   Ⓒ "part of the Earth not covered by water"

   Ⓓ "ground"

4. Which one is <u>not</u> a meaning of the word **bill**?

   Ⓐ "a piece of paper showing how much money someone owes"

   Ⓑ "the beak of a duck"

   Ⓒ "a green vegetable"

   Ⓓ "the beak of a goose"

5. Which sentence is <u>not</u> about a grassy area near a house?

   Ⓐ Tara and Anne have a sandbox in their yard.

   Ⓑ Our yard is not very big.

   Ⓒ We have a fence so that our dog cannot get out of the yard.

   Ⓓ I trained to run the 50-yard dash.

Homographs are words that are spelled the same but have different meanings.

You can wash your hands in a **sink**.
A rock will **sink** to the bottom of a lake.

Read each pair of sentences.
Match each sentence to the correct picture.

Elly likes to <u>brush</u> her teeth.

Dad dipped the <u>brush</u> in blue paint.

I hope my toy boat does not <u>sink</u>.

I always put my dishes in the <u>sink</u>.

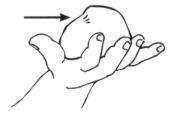

Kyle threw a <u>rock</u> into the lake.

Cammy will <u>rock</u> the baby to sleep.

That red <u>rose</u> has sharp thorns.

The sun <u>rose</u> over the mountains.

Homographs are words that are spelled the same but have different meanings.

A. Each sentence contains a pair of homographs.
Circle the homograph in the sentence that goes with the given meaning.

1. The sun <u>rose</u> over the <u>rose</u> garden.
Meaning: "went to a higher place"

2. The spoons always <u>sink</u> when I wash dishes in the <u>sink</u>.
Meaning: "to drop down underwater"

3. I <u>brush</u> my hair with a purple <u>brush</u>.
Meaning: "a tool with bristles and a handle"

B. Write your own sentences for each definition.

1. **sink**

"a place to wash": _____

_____

"to drop down underwater": _____

_____

2. **rock**

"a stone": _____

_____

"to move back and forth": _____

_____

Fill in the bubble next to the correct answer.

1. Which word has more than one meaning?

   Ⓐ brush

   Ⓑ toothpaste

   Ⓒ hair

   Ⓓ bath

2. Which word does not have more than one meaning?

   Ⓐ rock

   Ⓑ hat

   Ⓒ sink

   Ⓓ brush

3. Which one is not a meaning of the word **rock**?

   Ⓐ "a stone"

   Ⓑ "to move back and forth"

   Ⓒ "a way to move a baby"

   Ⓓ "hard"

4. Which one is not a meaning of the word **sink**?

   Ⓐ "a place to cook food"

   Ⓑ "to drop down underwater"

   Ⓒ "a place to wash your hands"

   Ⓓ "the opposite of **float**"

5. Which sentence is not about a flower?

   Ⓐ Mike watered the rosebush.

   Ⓑ Julie put the red rose in the blue vase.

   Ⓒ Kim thought the rose was beautiful.

   Ⓓ The moon rose high in the sky.

Homographs are words that are spelled the same but have different meanings.

> If you did a good job on something, you did it **well**.
> You can get water from a **well**.

A. Circle the sentence that goes with each picture.

Queen Mary was a fair <u>ruler</u>.

Mary used a <u>ruler</u> to measure a pen.

James got a <u>present</u> for his birthday.

James was <u>present</u> in class today.

Jack got water from the <u>well</u>.

Jack did <u>well</u> on the math test.

Sarah climbed <u>down</u> the ladder.

Sarah's pillow is made of <u>down</u>.

B. Circle the definition that goes with the sentence.

1. Pedro rode his bike <u>down</u> the hill.
   - the opposite of **up**
   - small, soft feathers

2. Tanya was <u>present</u> for the test.
   - a gift
   - to be at a certain place

Homographs are words that are spelled the same but have different meanings.

A. Read each sentence.
   Write the meaning of the underlined homograph.

1. Karen stayed home from school until she felt <u>well</u>.

   meaning: _____

   Dan used a bucket to get water from the <u>well</u>.

   meaning: _____

2. King Edward was loved by the people because he was a fair <u>ruler</u>.

   meaning: _____

   Jenny used a <u>ruler</u> to draw a straight line.

   meaning: _____

B. Write sentences using homographs.

1. Use **present**, meaning "gift."

   _____

   _____

2. Use **down**, the opposite of **up**.

   _____

   _____

Fill in the bubble next to the correct answer.

1. Which word does <u>not</u> have more than one meaning?

Ⓐ well

Ⓑ down

Ⓒ up

Ⓓ ruler

2. Which one is <u>not</u> a meaning of the word **well**?

Ⓐ "good"

Ⓑ "a place to get diamonds"

Ⓒ "a place to get water"

Ⓓ "not sick"

3. Which one gives two meanings of the word **down**?

Ⓐ "pillow," "slide"

Ⓑ "not up," "feathers"

Ⓒ "sink," "float"

Ⓓ "jacket," "stairs"

4. Which sentence is about the leader of a country?

Ⓐ I used a ruler to measure my foot.

Ⓑ The principal buys the school rulers.

Ⓒ King Harold was the ruler of Fabulasia for 50 years.

Ⓓ My ruler is made of wood.

5. Which sentence is <u>not</u> about a gift?

Ⓐ I picked out a special present for my friend Amber.

Ⓑ I wrapped Amber's present in blue and red paper.

Ⓒ I was present at Amber's birthday party.

Ⓓ Amber said she liked the present I got her.

Homographs are words that are spelled the same but have different meanings.

You can turn **left** at the corner.
You may have **left** your book at home.

Read each sentence.
Match the <u>underlined</u> homograph with its meaning in the box.
Write the letter on the line.

> a. to be lazy
> b. a baked shape

1. _____ Buy a <u>loaf</u> of wheat bread at the store.

2. _____ My family likes to <u>loaf</u> around on Saturday mornings.

> a. a carnival
> b. follows the rules

3. _____ We rode the Ferris wheel at the <u>fair</u>.

4. _____ I thought the game was not <u>fair</u>.

> a. opposite of **heavy**
> b. opposite of **dark**

5. _____ During summer, we stay outside as long as it's <u>light</u>.

6. _____ My backpack was easy to carry because it was so <u>light</u>.

Name: _____

Homographs are words that are spelled the same but have different meanings.

Use each homograph in a sentence. Make sure that your sentence fits the definition.

1. **fair**

   "a carnival": _____

   _____

   "follows the rules": _____

   _____

2. **light**

   "not dark": _____

   _____

   "not heavy": _____

   _____

3. **left**

   "past tense of **leave**": _____

   _____

   "opposite of **right**": _____

   _____

Fill in the bubble next to the correct answer.

1. Homographs are words that are spelled _____.

    Ⓐ differently but have the same meaning

    Ⓑ differently and have different meanings

    Ⓒ the same but have different meanings

    Ⓓ the same and have the same meaning

2. Which one is <u>not</u> a meaning of the word **fair**?

    Ⓐ "a carnival"

    Ⓑ "a place with rides and animals"

    Ⓒ "to treat someone unkindly"

    Ⓓ "to play by following the rules"

3. Which one is <u>not</u> a meaning of the word **light**?

    Ⓐ "yellow"

    Ⓑ "not dark"

    Ⓒ "not heavy"

    Ⓓ "easy to lift"

4. Which sentence is about being lazy?

    Ⓐ Mom cut a slice from the loaf of bread.

    Ⓑ When the dough rises, the loaf is ready to bake.

    Ⓒ Nicky went to the store for a loaf of bread.

    Ⓓ My dad and brother like to loaf in front of the TV.

5. Which sentence is <u>not</u> about leaving something?

    Ⓐ I left my pencil on the desk.

    Ⓑ I write with my left hand.

    Ⓒ Todd left his little brother behind.

    Ⓓ I left two cookies for my sister.

A **prefix** is a word part added to the beginning of a base word. Adding a prefix changes the word's meaning.

The prefix **un–** means "not" or "the opposite of."

un– + welcome = **unwelcome** ("not wanted")
un– + pack = **unpack** ("the opposite of **pack**")

Add the prefix **un–** to make each new word.
Then circle the sentence that describes it.

1. _____pack
   a. I put my clothes in the suitcase.
   b. I took my clothes out of the suitcase.

2. _____kind
   a. That girl pushed me down.
   b. That girl helped me when I fell down.

3. _____sure
   a. I know the answer to the question.
   b. I do not know the answer to the question.

4. _____afraid
   a. That big dog is friendly and playful.
   b. That big dog might bite me!

5. _____hurt
   a. I fell down and skinned my knee.
   b. I fell down, but I am okay.

6. _____clear
   a. That game is hard to understand.
   b. That game is easy to play.

Name: _____

A **prefix** is a word part added to the beginning of a base word. Adding a prefix changes the word's meaning.

The prefix **un–** means "not" or "the opposite of."

Add the prefix **un–** to each bold word.
Then write a sentence using the new word.

1. **wanted:** _____ = "not wanted"

_____

_____

2. **important:** _____ = "not important"

_____

_____

3. **healthy:** _____ = "not healthy"

_____

_____

4. **welcome:** _____ = "not welcome"

_____

_____

Name: _____

A **prefix** is a word part added to the beginning of a base word. Adding a prefix changes the word's meaning.

Add **un–** to each word in the box. Think about the meanings. Then choose the best word for each blank in the story.

> _____hurt   _____kind   _____sure   _____afraid
>
> _____healthy   _____welcome   _____pack

My family went on a picnic today! At first we were _____

we would go because it looked like rain. But then the sky cleared up, and

the sun came out.

At the park, my sister and I raced to the picnic table. I slipped and fell,

but I was _____. Then I helped _____

the picnic basket. We had sandwiches, watermelon, carrot sticks, and

brownies. Some people say brownies are _____, but

Dad makes them with whole-wheat flour and honey.

We had some _____ guests while we were eating.

Lots of ants came! My sister was scared that they might bite her. I was

_____. I knew that they were not the kind that bite. She

wanted to smash the ants. Dad said that would be _____.

The park is their home, not ours.

A **prefix** is a word part added to the beginning of a base word. Adding a prefix changes the word's meaning.

The prefix **re–** means "again."

re– + use = **reuse** ("to use again")
re– + start = **restart** ("to start again")

Add the prefix **re–** to make a new word.
Then match the new word to the sentence that describes it.

1. _____ fill   •

    _____ read   •

    _____ tell   •

    _____ stack   •

    • The cans fell over, so I stacked them again.

    • I asked Dad to tell me the story again.

    • The book was so good that I read it a second time.

    • The pitcher was empty, so I filled it again.

2. _____ write   •

    _____ do   •

    _____ build   •

    _____ check   •

    • I built my sand castle back up after it fell down.

    • I always check my work twice before I turn it in.

    • I will write my paper over and fix the mistakes.

    • I lost my homework, so I had to do it again.

 Vocabulary Fundamentals • EMC 2802 • © Evan-Moor Corp.

A **prefix** is a word part added to the beginning of
a base word. Adding a prefix changes the word's meaning.

The prefix **re–** means "again."

A. Write the meaning of each word.

1. **recheck:** _____

2. **restack:** _____

3. **reuse:** _____

4. **restart:** _____

B. Finish each sentence.

1. I had to <u>rewrite</u> my paper because _____

_____.

2. We will <u>review</u> the new spelling words because _____

_____.

3. Kim had to <u>refill</u> the ice tray because _____

_____.

4. We had to <u>rebuild</u> the snow fort because _____

_____.

5. My sister asked me to <u>reread</u> the story because _____

_____.

Fill in the bubble next to the correct answer.

1. The prefix **re–** means _____ .

   Ⓐ "at"

   Ⓑ "again"

   Ⓒ "always"

   Ⓓ "above"

2. Which word means "to check again"?

   Ⓐ checker

   Ⓑ checkout

   Ⓒ uncheck

   Ⓓ recheck

3. If you did your homework incorrectly, what would you need to do?

   Ⓐ redo it

   Ⓑ refill it

   Ⓒ reuse it

   Ⓓ rearrange it

4. Which word does <u>not</u> contain the prefix **re–**?

   Ⓐ restack

   Ⓑ rewrite

   Ⓒ restful

   Ⓓ review

5. Which sentence is written correctly?

   Ⓐ I had to reread the test question.

   Ⓑ I had to read the retest question.

   Ⓒ I had to read the test requestion.

   Ⓓ I rehad to read the test question.

Name: _____

A **prefix** is a word part added to the beginning of
a base word. Adding a prefix changes the word's meaning.

The prefix **dis–** means "not" or "the opposite of."

dis– + connected = **disconnected** ("not connected")
dis– + believe = **disbelieve** ("the opposite of **believe**")

Add the prefix **dis–** to make a new word.
Then circle the sentence that describes it.

1. _____agree

    a. We both feel the same way about it.

    b. Each of us feels differently about it.

2. _____like

    a. I do not enjoy doing math problems.

    b. I enjoy doing math problems.

3. _____continue

    a. I stopped reading the book.

    b. I kept reading the book.

4. _____obey

    a. I followed the teacher's directions.

    b. I did not follow the teacher's directions.

5. _____interest

    a. I do not want to learn more.

    b. I want to learn more.

6. _____trust

    a. I know she is telling the truth.

    b. I think she might be lying.

A **prefix** is a word part added to the beginning of a base word. Adding a prefix changes the word's meaning.

The prefix **dis–** means "not" or "the opposite of."

Add the prefix **dis–** to the underlined word in each sentence. Then rewrite the sentence with the new word.

1. Mike's desk was in <u>order</u>. _____order

   _____

2. Lily wants to <u>connect</u> the wires. _____connect

   _____

3. Mom <u>approves</u> of eating in the living room. _____approves

   _____

   _____

4. I really <u>like</u> spinach and cabbage. _____like

   _____

   _____

5. The magician made the rabbit <u>appear</u>. _____appear

   _____

   _____

 Vocabulary Fundamentals • EMC 2802 • © Evan-Moor Corp.

A **prefix** is a word part added to the beginning of
a base word. Adding a prefix changes the word's meaning.

Add **dis**– to each word in the box. Think about the meanings.
Then choose the best word for each blank in the story.

_____agree   _____obeys   _____like

_____appears   _____approves   _____continue

    My new puppy, Junior, is a big problem! I know he's smart, but he

never does what I say. If I call him to come in from the yard, he

_____ and _____ into the bushes.

He barks all the time and has even dug up our flower bed. I know our

neighbor, Mrs. Jones, _____ of his behavior.

    "Junior is a bad dog!" I told my dad.

    "I _____," said Dad. "If we want Junior to

_____ doing things we _____, we

have to teach him what to do."

    Dad got a book on dog training, and we worked with Junior every

day. He was a quick learner. Soon, he was the best-behaved dog

on our block!

A **prefix** is a word part added to the beginning of
a base word. Adding a prefix changes the word's meaning.

The prefix **pre–** means "before."

pre– + pay = **prepay** ("to pay before")
pre– + heat = **preheat** ("to heat before")

A. Underline the prefix in each sentence.
Then write the base word on the line.

1. Be sure to preheat the oven.   pre + _____

2. We had to prepay to buy our tickets.   pre + _____

3. My little sister goes to preschool.   pre + _____

4. We watched the preflight safety movie.   pre + _____

5. The paper was precut for our art project.   pre + _____

B. Add the prefix **pre–** to make a new word.
Then match the new word to the sentence that describes it.

1. _____ board   •   • The flour and the salt were already
                                 combined.

2. _____ view   •   • People with small children get on
                                 the plane first.

3. _____ mix   •   • I put on safety goggles before the
                                 experiment.

4. _____ caution •   • We saw the movie before anyone else.

A **prefix** is a word part added to the beginning of
a base word. Adding a prefix changes the word's meaning.

The prefix **pre–** means "before."

A. Complete each sentence with a word from the box.

prepay	prerecorded	preview	preheat
prebaked	prepackaged	preschool	precaution

1. Timmy got to finger-paint in _____ today.

2. The recipe said to _____ the oven.

3. We watched the _____ baseball game on TV.

4. The rolls were _____, so we only had to warm them.

5. It costs less to get into the fair if you _____.

6. The _____ cookies are either in boxes or paper bags.

7. We watched a movie _____ before the main show.

8. Amber took the _____ of wearing a life vest.

B. Use a word from the box to write a sentence of your own.

_____

_____

_____

Name: _____

Fill in the bubble next to the correct answer.

1. Which word has a prefix that means "before"?

Ⓐ precut

Ⓑ uncut

Ⓒ undercut

Ⓓ cutting

2. Which word means "to pay ahead of time"?

Ⓐ paid

Ⓑ overpay

Ⓒ prepay

Ⓓ payment

3. Which word means "to let the oven get hot before you bake something"?

Ⓐ premix

Ⓑ preview

Ⓒ prebake

Ⓓ preheat

4. Which word does not contain the prefix **pre–**?

Ⓐ precaution

Ⓑ president

Ⓒ prerecorded

Ⓓ prepackaged

5. Which sentence tells about a man boarding a plane before anyone else?

Ⓐ The man was permitted to preboard the plane.

Ⓑ The man was permitted to reboard the plane.

Ⓒ The man was permitted to unboard the plane.

Ⓓ The man was permitted to disboard the plane.

Vocabulary Fundamentals • EMC 2802 • © Evan-Moor Corp.

A **prefix** is a word part added to the beginning of a base word. Adding a prefix changes the word's meaning.

The prefix **mis–** means "bad" or "wrong."

mis– + behavior = **misbehavior** ("bad behavior")
mis– + count = **miscount** ("to count incorrectly")

A. Add the prefix **mis–** to each <u>underlined</u> word.
Write the new word on the line.

1. to <u>lead</u> someone in the wrong direction   _____

2. to <u>count</u> something incorrectly   _____

3. to <u>judge</u> someone wrongly   _____

4. to be badly <u>informed</u>   _____

5. to <u>pronounce</u> a word incorrectly   _____

6. to put something in the wrong <u>place</u>   _____

B. Circle the word in each sentence that has a prefix.
Then write the base word on the line.

1. I try not to (misspell) words.   mis + _spell_____

2. We will be late if I misplace the keys.   mis + _____

3. I never misbehave in school.   mis + _____

4. Add carefully so you do not miscalculate the answer.   mis + _____

Name: _____

A **prefix** is a word part added to the beginning of
a base word. Adding a prefix changes the word's meaning.

The prefix **mis–** means "bad" or "wrong."

A. Write the word from the box to match each definition.

misplace	misspell	mislabel
misbehave	mismatch	mistreat

1. to put on the wrong label   _____

2. to spell **cat** this way: k-a-t   _____

3. to throw popcorn at a movie   _____

4. to pair a red sock with a blue one   _____

5. to forget where you put something   _____

6. to be mean to someone or something   _____

B. Use each word in a sentence.

1. **misbehave:** _____

_____

2. **miscalculate:** _____

_____

3. **misunderstand:** _____

_____

A **prefix** is a word part added to the beginning of a base word. Adding a prefix changes the word's meaning.

Add the prefix **mis–** to each word in the box. Think about the meanings. Then choose the best word for each blank in the story.

_____ placed   _____judged   _____ treated   _____ match

_____ calculated _____ pronounce _____ understand _____ behaving

My family is from Mexico. When we first came to the United States, I did

not know very much English. Whenever I talked to someone, I would often

_____ a lot of words. Sometimes, other kids would

_____ me. It was hard to make friends.

A boy named Kyle _____ me because I was different.

One day, the teacher caught him _____. She said that

we had to learn to get along. She made us work together in math. What

a _____! At first, Kyle got angry at me because I

_____ my pencil and had to borrow his. Then things

got better. I saw that Kyle made a lot of mistakes on a test. He had

_____ some of the subtraction problems. I showed him

an easy way to do them. That made him happy. Soon, Kyle and I became

friends! He said he was sorry for being mean to me and that he had

_____ me.

A **prefix** is a word part added to the beginning of a base word. Adding a prefix changes the word's meaning.

The prefix **over–** means "too much."

over– + pay = **overpay** ("to pay too much")
over– + weight = **overweight** ("to weigh too much")

A. Add the prefix **over–** to make a new word.
   Then match the new word to its meaning.

1. _____cook •   • to pay too much

2. _____do •   • to spend too much

3. _____pay •   • to cook too much

4. _____spend •   • to do too much

B. Circle each word with a prefix.
   Then write the prefix and the base word on the lines.

1. Dad was tired and overworked.   _____ + _____

2. That library book is overdue.   _____ + _____

3. Try not to overload the wheelbarrow.   _____ + _____

4. The room was overcrowded.   _____ + _____

5. If you overwater the plant, it might die. _____ + _____

6. It is hard not to overeat at a party. _____ + _____

   Vocabulary Fundamentals • EMC 2802 • © Evan-Moor Corp.

A **prefix** is a word part added to the beginning of
a base word. Adding a prefix changes the word's meaning.

The prefix **over–** means "too much."

A. Complete each sentence with a word from the box.

overload	overdue	overdo	overactive
overcrowded	overcook	overspend	overwater

1. Dad did not want to _____ in order to buy a new car.

2. It's hard to get my _____ little brother to sit still for a meal.

3. I must go to the library today because my book is _____ .

4. On your first hike, don't _____ it by walking too far.

5. It is easy to _____ a cactus plant.

6. If you _____ your backpack, it will be hard to carry.

7. The desks were wall-to-wall in the _____ classroom.

8. If you _____ the meat, it will get tough.

B. Use a word from the box to write a sentence of your own.

_____

_____

Name: _____

Fill in the bubble next to the correct answer.

1. A prefix is a word part _____.

   Ⓐ added to the end of a base word to make a new word

   Ⓑ added to the beginning of a base word to make a new word

   Ⓒ added to the middle of a base word to make a new word

   Ⓓ that sounds like another word

2. Which of these means "to cook something too much"?

   Ⓐ precook

   Ⓑ recook

   Ⓒ overcook

   Ⓓ miscook

3. If a bus is so full that people are standing up, the bus is _____.

   Ⓐ discrowded

   Ⓑ uncrowded

   Ⓒ miscrowded

   Ⓓ overcrowded

4. If your father gives you $500 to mow the lawn, you have been _____.

   Ⓐ overpaid

   Ⓑ unpaid

   Ⓒ mispaid

   Ⓓ repaid

5. Which sentence is written correctly?

   Ⓐ If you reload a box, it could be too heavy to lift.

   Ⓑ If you preload a box, it could be too heavy to lift.

   Ⓒ If you overload a box, it could be too heavy to lift.

   Ⓓ If you unload a box, it could be too heavy to lift.

A **prefix** is a word part added to the beginning of
a base word. Adding a prefix changes the word's meaning.

The prefix **under–** means "beneath" or "not enough."

under– + water = **underwater** ("beneath the water")
under– + charge = **undercharge** ("to not charge enough")

A. Add the prefix **under–** to each base word.
Then match the new word to its meaning.

1. _____ground •   • not cooked enough

2. _____fed •   • underwear

3. _____paid •   • below the ground

4. _____line •   • not given enough food

5. _____cooked •   • not paid enough

6. _____shirt •   • to draw a line beneath

B. Fill in each blank with a word from above.

1. I did not want to eat the _____ hamburger.

2. The teacher said to _____ our spelling words
in the sentences.

3. Dad wears an _____ every day.

4. We could tell the kitten was _____, because it was so thin.

5. _____ pipes bring water to your home.

6. Tony asked for more money because he was being _____.

A **prefix** is a word part added to the beginning of
a base word. Adding a prefix changes the word's meaning.

The prefix **under–** means "beneath" or "not enough."

A. Fill in each blank with a word from the box.

> underfoot   underline   underwater   underpriced   undercover

1. If you draw a line beneath a word, you _____ it.

2. If something is being sold for less than it is worth,

   it is _____ .

3. If you keep tripping on something, it is _____ .

4. A deep-sea diver swims _____ .

5. The detective went _____ to catch a thief.

B. Use each word in a sentence.

1. **underwater:** _____

   _____

2. **underpriced:** _____

   _____

3. **underfoot:** _____

   _____

A **prefix** is a word part added to the beginning of a base word. Adding a prefix changes the word's meaning.

Add the prefix **under–** to each word in the box. Think about the meanings. Then choose the best word for each blank in the story.

_____ lined   _____ foot   _____ cooked

_____ ground   _____ priced   _____ cover

Today, my mom took me with her to the grocery store. First, my mom

got a pound of ground beef. The butcher reminded her to cook it for at least

ten minutes so it would not be _____.

Then, Mom got out her pen and _____ three things

on the shopping list. She gave the list to me and sent me off to find them. I

pretended to be an _____ secret agent looking for clues.

The first thing I found was the carrots. (I think it is neat how carrots grow

_____.) Then, I went to look for bread. I picked an

_____ loaf that was on sale. I got the milk next and then

met my mom at the checkout.

On the way to our car, I tripped on a rock that was

_____ and scraped my knee. Luckily, we had bought

bandages at the store!

Name: _____

A **suffix** is a word part added to the end of a base word. Adding a suffix makes a new word.

The suffixes **–er** and **–or** mean "a person who."

teach + **–er** = **teacher** ("a person who teaches")
sail + **–or** = **sailor** ("a person who sails")

A. Read each word. Circle the suffix.
   Match the word to the correct picture.

1. baker •

2. sailor •

3. player •

4. farmer •

B. Complete each sentence with one of the four words from above.

1. The first _____ to get 50 points wins.

2. My grandmother is the best pie _____ .

3. The _____ will steer the boat.

4. The _____ grew tomatoes to sell at the market.

A **suffix** is a word part added to the end of a base word. Adding a suffix makes a new word.

The suffixes **–er** and **–or** mean "a person who."

Choose the correct **–er** or **–or** word from the box to answer each riddle.

> painter   actor   pitcher   server   doctor
> builder   worker   author   inventor   operator

1. You see me when you watch movies. Who am I?   _____

2. I bring you food at a restaurant. Who am I?   _____

3. I think up new things. Who am I?   _____

4. I can make your house a new color. Who am I?   _____

5. I can be any person who does a job. Who am I?   _____

6. You can thank me for your favorite book. Who am I?   _____

7. I can make new houses. Who am I?   _____

8. I'll throw the ball to you. Who am I?   _____

9. I help you to make phone calls. Who am I?   _____

10. You visit me if you are sick. Who am I?   _____

Fill in the bubble next to the correct answer.

1. A suffix is a word part _____.

   Ⓐ added to the beginning of a base word

   Ⓑ added to the end of a base word

   Ⓒ that is a word by itself

   Ⓓ that makes a compound word

2. Which two suffixes mean "a person who"?

   Ⓐ –er, –ed

   Ⓑ –or, –ar

   Ⓒ –er, –or

   Ⓓ –or, –ur

3. The word **farmer** means _____.

   Ⓐ "a place where vegetables are grown"

   Ⓑ "a person who works on a farm"

   Ⓒ "about the same as **barn**"

   Ⓓ "a person who sells things"

4. Which word does <u>not</u> name a person who does something?

   Ⓐ author

   Ⓑ doctor

   Ⓒ actor

   Ⓓ elevator

5. Which word best completes this sentence?
   The 911 _____ sent the fire engines to the burning building.

   Ⓐ inventor

   Ⓑ server

   Ⓒ operator

   Ⓓ teacher

A **suffix** is a word part added to the end of a base word. Adding a suffix makes a new word.

The suffix **–ful** means "full of."

color + **–ful** = **colorful** ("full of color")
pain + **–ful** = **painful** ("full of pain")

A. Use the suffix **–ful** to make a word for each definition.

1. full of care _____   5. full of delight _____

2. full of cheer _____   6. full of color _____

3. full of help _____   7. full of skill _____

4. full of power _____   8. full of pain _____

B. Complete each sentence with a word from above.

1. Tim used the _____ backhoe to move the rocks.

2. Doing the dishes is one way to be _____ at home.

3. Katie used a lot of crayons to draw a _____ picture.

4. The sunny day put everyone in a _____ mood.

5. Andy took a _____ fall off his bike.

6. Everyone had a _____ time at the party.

7. Scott is a _____ soccer player because he practices.

8. Adults should be _____ when lighting a fire.

A **suffix** is a word part added to the end of a base word.
Adding a suffix makes a new word.

The suffix **–ful** means "full of."

Add the suffix –**ful** to each base word.
Then write a sentence with the new word.

1. thank_____

_____

_____

2. help_____

_____

_____

3. play_____

_____

_____

4. use_____

_____

_____

5. forget_____

_____

_____

A **suffix** is a word part added to the end of a base word.
Adding a suffix makes a new word.

Add **–ful** to each word in the box. Think about the meanings.
Then choose the best word for each blank in the story.

play_____   thank_____   care_____   skill_____

color_____   cheer_____   thought_____   use_____

My aunt gave me a big box of colored pencils for my birthday. She knows

I want to be an artist when I grow up, so it was a _____ gift.

I told her how _____ I was to have so many colored pencils.

She told me that if I work hard, I will be a _____ artist

someday.

I decided to draw a _____ picture for my aunt. I drew

a kitten playing with a ball of yarn. I tried to be _____ with

my new pencils, but I broke one of the tips. Luckily, there was a sharpener

in the box. I break pencil tips a lot, so I know that sharpener will be very

_____ .

My aunt loved the picture! She said she would put it in her kitchen

because seeing that _____ kitten would put her in

a _____ mood every morning.

A **suffix** is a word part added to the end of a base word.
Adding a suffix makes a new word.

The suffix **–less** means "without."

fear + **–less** = **fearless** ("without fear")
worth + **–less** = **worthless** ("without worth")

Add the suffix **–less** to make a new word.
Then circle the sentence that describes it.

1. pain_____
   a. It hurt a lot.
   b. It did not hurt at all.

2. sleep_____
   a. I could not fall asleep.
   b. I slept all night long.

3. thought_____
   a. She never thinks about other people.
   b. She always thinks about other people.

4. use_____
   a. We used it every day.
   b. It was broken, so we never used it.

5. harm_____
   a. That dog would never bite anyone.
   b. That dog bit someone yesterday.

6. tire_____
   a. The men stopped to rest.
   b. The men marched all night long.

Name: _____

A **suffix** is a word part added to the end of a base word. Adding a suffix makes a new word.

The suffix **–less** means "without."

Replace the <u>underlined</u> phrase with a word that ends with the suffix **–less**. Rewrite each sentence.

1. The computer was so old that it was <u>without worth</u>.

   _____

   _____

2. The boring movie seemed to be <u>without end</u>.

   _____

   _____

3. I was afraid, but my brother was <u>without fear</u>.

   _____

   _____

4. The diamond was so big that it was <u>without a price</u>.

   _____

   _____

5. I was <u>without care</u> when I broke my friend's robot.

   _____

   _____

Fill in the bubble next to the correct answer.

1. The suffix **–less** means _____ .

    Ⓐ "full of"

    Ⓑ "less than"

    Ⓒ "already"

    Ⓓ "without"

2. Which word means "without hope"?

    Ⓐ hopeful

    Ⓑ hoped

    Ⓒ hopeless

    Ⓓ hoping

3. Which word does <u>not</u> contain the suffix **–less**?

    Ⓐ endless

    Ⓑ bless

    Ⓒ sleepless

    Ⓓ priceless

4. Which sentence is written correctly?

    Ⓐ The broken hammer was using.

    Ⓑ The broken hammer was useless.

    Ⓒ The broken hammer was user.

    Ⓓ The broken hammer was useness.

5. Which of these is the correct way to divide the word **thoughtless** into a base word and a suffix?

    Ⓐ though | tless

    Ⓑ thoughtl | ess

    Ⓒ thought | less

    Ⓓ thou | ghtless

A **suffix** is a word part added to the end of a base word.
Adding a suffix makes a new word.

The suffix **–ness** means "state of being."

sad + **–ness** = **sadness** ("state of being sad")
great + **–ness** = **greatness** ("state of being great")

A. Circle the word with the suffix **–ness** in each sentence.

1. Mrs. Tyler was always helpful and was known for her kindness.

2. Ben was looking forward to the softness of his bed after the camping trip.

3. Cody shined his flashlight into the darkness.

4. Anna's sickness lasted for a long time.

5. Spelling was Maria's weakness, but she was good at math.

6. The brightness of the morning light made Kevin squint.

7. David said he was sorry and asked for forgiveness.

8. Mom says that politeness is always important.

B. Divide each word you circled above into a base word
   and a suffix.

1. _____ + _____   5. _____ + _____

2. _____ + _____   6. _____ + _____

3. _____ + _____   7. _____ + _____

4. _____ + _____   8. _____ + _____

Name: _____

A **suffix** is a word part added to the end of a base word.
Adding a suffix makes a new word.

The suffix **–ness** means "state of being."

Fill in the first blank with the best word from the box.
Then complete the sentence with your own words.

> foolishness   sickness   forgiveness   darkness   sadness   softness

1. Kate asked her mom for _____ because she had

   lied about _____.

2. Lucy went out into the _____ to search for _____

   _____.

3. Mom says it is _____ to spend a lot of money on

   _____.

4. Tom felt _____ because his dog _____

   _____.

5. Tasha's _____ caused her to miss _____

   _____.

6. The _____ of the blanket felt wonderful after _____

   _____.

Name: _____

A **suffix** is a word part added to the end of a base word.
Adding a suffix makes a new word.

Add the suffix **–ness** to each word in the box. Think about the
meanings. Then choose the best word for each blank in the story.

soft_____	kind_____	bright_____	dark_____
sick_____	sad_____	foolish_____	weak_____

When Emily woke up this morning, she felt hot and her head hurt. When

she tried to stand up, she felt _____ in her legs, and she

nearly fell over. Emily sank back into the _____ of her bed.

Mom came in and pulled back the curtains. The _____ of

the morning sun hurt Emily's eyes. Mom quickly shut the curtains, and there

was _____ again. Mom felt Emily's head and said that Emily

was sick. She would need to stay in bed all day and rest. Emily felt

_____. She had wanted to play with her friend Kim that day.

Later, Kim brought over a get-well card for Emily. Kim wanted to give it to

Emily herself, but Emily's mom said that would be _____

because then Kim might catch the _____ herself. A few

days later, Emily felt all better! When she saw Kim again, she thanked her

for the card and for her _____.

WORD PLAY

Twenty pages of fun activities, including:

- word scrambles
- analogies
- categories
- word ladders
- rhyming riddles

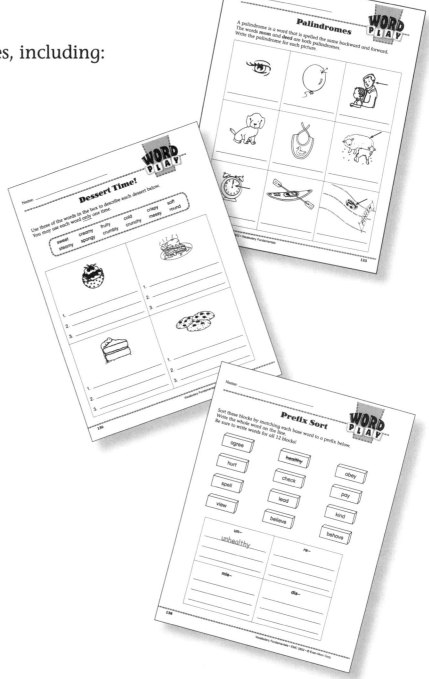

Name: _____

Palindromes

A palindrome is a word that is spelled the same backward and forward.
The words **mom** and **deed** are both palindromes.
Write the palindrome for each picture.

_____	_____	_____
_____	_____	_____
_____	_____	_____

Name: _____

Where Do You Find It?

A. Read each set of words.
   Add one more word.
   Then tell where you would find each set.

1. swings, seesaw, monkey bars, _____

   Where do you find them? _____

2. desks, pencils, students, _____

   Where do you find them? _____

3. sink, spoons, mixing bowls, _____

   Where do you find them? _____

4. carrots, soil, seeds, _____

   Where do you find them? _____

5. cars, stop signs, crosswalks, _____

   Where do you find them? _____

6. seats, radio, keys, _____

   Where do you find them? _____

B. Write your own set of words.
   Have a friend add one more word. Then answer the question.

   _____, _____, _____

   New word: _____

   Where do you find them? _____

Vocabulary Fundamentals • EMC 2802 • © Evan-Moor Corp.

Name: _____

Color Scramble

A. Unscramble the name of each color. Write the letters on the lines.

1. l e a t   ___ ___ [ ] ___

2. s e o r   [ ] ___ ___ ___

3. y g a r   ___ ___ [ ] ___

4. t v o l e i   ___ [ ] ___ ___ ___ ___

5. a g e m a n t ___ ___ ___ ___ [ ] ___ ___

6. u b e l   [ ] ___ ___ ___

7. o a r l c   ___ [ ] ___ ___ ___

8. l o l w e y ___ ___ ___ ___ ___ [ ]

B. Start with the top box above.
   Write the letters on the lines to answer the riddle.

What bow cannot be tied?

___ ___ ___ ___ ___ ___ ___ ___ ___

Name: _____

Dessert Time!

Use three of the words in the box to describe each dessert below.
You may use each word <u>only</u> one time.

sweet	creamy	fruity	cold	crispy	soft
steamy	spongy	crumbly	crunchy	messy	round

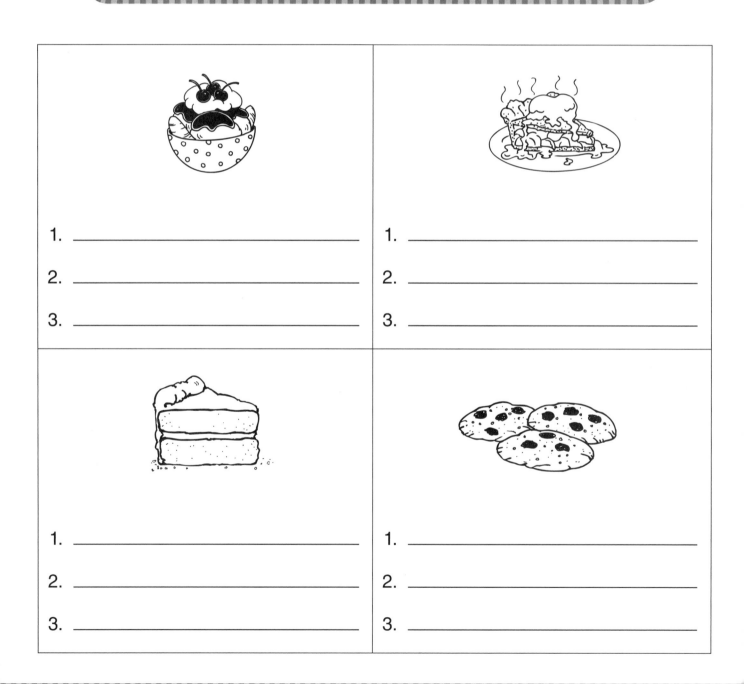

1. _____

2. _____

3. _____

1. _____

2. _____

3. _____

1. _____

2. _____

3. _____

1. _____

2. _____

3. _____

Vocabulary Fundamentals • EMC 2802 • © Evan-Moor Corp.

Name: _____

Analogies Around the House

Analogies tell how one pair of things relates to another pair. Choose the correct word and write it on the line to complete each analogy.

1. **Bed** is to **sleeping** as **chair** is to _____.
   (table, sitting, wood)

2. **TV** is to **watching** as **book** is to _____.
   (reading, words, story)

3. **Stove** is to **hot** as **freezer** is to _____.
   (big, kitchen, cold)

4. **Tape** is to **sticky** as **rubber band** is to _____.
   (stretchy, soft, long)

5. **Pillow** is to **soft** as **table** is to _____.
   (wood, hard, dinner)

6. **Stove** is to **kitchen** as **tub** is to _____.
   (water, bath, bathroom)

7. **Picture** is to **wall** as **curtain** is to _____.
   (window, mirror, fabric)

8. **Sponge** is to **washing** as **broom** is to _____.
   (handle, brush, sweeping)

Name: _____

Prefix Sort

Sort these blocks by matching each base word to a prefix below.
Write the whole word on the line.
Be sure to write words for all 12 blocks!

agree	healthy	obey
hurt	check	pay
spell	lead	kind
view	believe	behave

un–	re–
__unhealthy__	_____
_____	_____
_____	_____
mis–	**dis–**
_____	_____
_____	_____
_____	_____

 Vocabulary Fundamentals • EMC 2802 • © Evan-Moor Corp.

The Great Wall

The Great Wall of China is thousands of miles long. It was built many years ago to keep invaders out of China. Follow the directions below to find another interesting fact about the wall.

massive	it	undo	took	friendly	bluebird
unread	hallway	over	baseball	a	sickness
million	sadness	huge	people	unknown	vast
large	to	kindness	outside	build	kind
softness	untie	the	pleasant	giant	wall

1. Cross out all the compound words.
2. Cross out all the synonyms for the word **big**.
3. Cross out all the words with the suffix **–ness**.
4. Cross out all the words with the prefix **un–**.
5. Cross out all the synonyms for **nice**.
6. Write the remaining words on the lines.

_____

_____

Name: _____

Hopping Home

It takes Robby Rabbit a long time to get home to his mother. He only hops on compound words! Color the stones that Robby hops on.

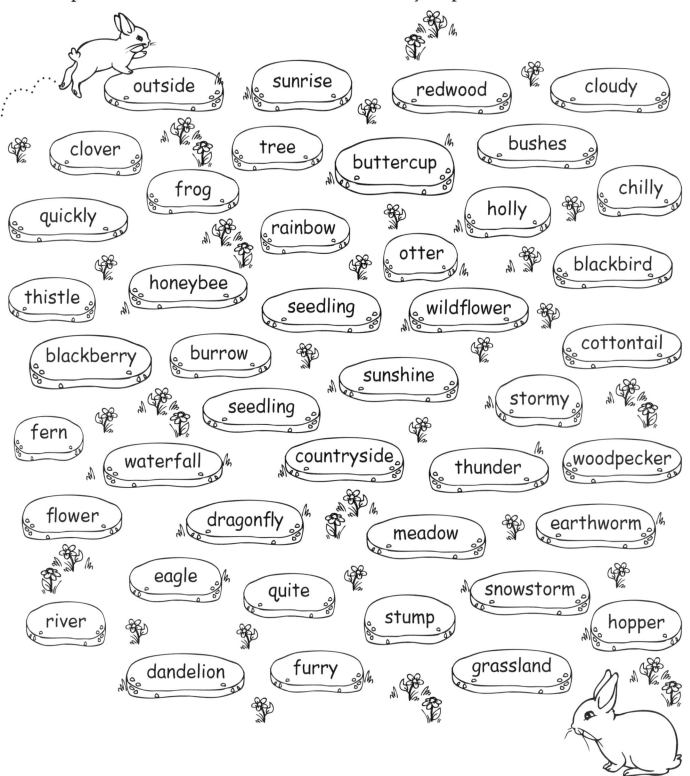

outside · sunrise · redwood · cloudy · clover · tree · buttercup · bushes · frog · chilly · quickly · rainbow · holly · otter · blackbird · thistle · honeybee · seedling · wildflower · blackberry · burrow · cottontail · sunshine · stormy · seedling · fern · waterfall · countryside · thunder · woodpecker · flower · dragonfly · meadow · earthworm · eagle · quite · snowstorm · river · stump · hopper · dandelion · furry · grassland

Vocabulary Fundamentals • EMC 2802 • © Evan-Moor Corp.

Name: _____

Apple Harvest

Sort the apples into the pails by matching each base word with a suffix.

- If the word goes with the suffix **–less**, write it in the **–less** pail.
- If the word goes with **–ful**, write it in the **–ful** pail.
- Write words that can go with both suffixes in the overlapping part of the pails.

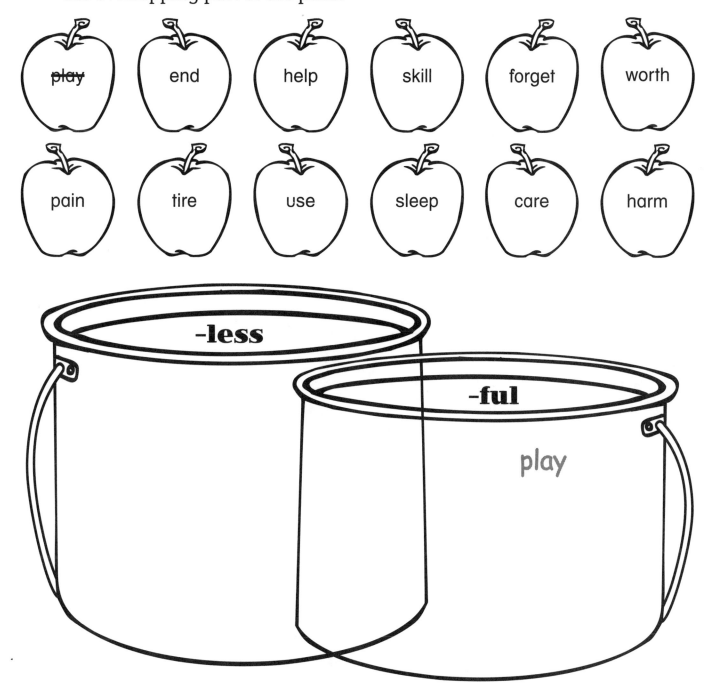

Name: _____

What has...

A. Can you find the answer to the riddle below?
   Use the clues to fill in the boxes.
   For each new word, change only the letter in the shaded box.
   The word you write in the last row is the answer.

Clues	k	i	c	k
to choose				
you do this before you go on a trip				
a good place for a picnic				
not the whole thing				
what a tired dog does				
a piece of glass in a window				
a stick used for walking				
what you eat ice cream in				
to arrive or enter				
What has teeth but does not have a mouth?				

B. Circle the picture that shows your answer.

   Vocabulary Fundamentals • EMC 2802 • © Evan-Moor Corp.

Name: _____

Odd Animal Out

A. Circle the animal that does <u>not</u> belong.
   Then tell why.

1. turtle   lizard   fox   rattlesnake

   _____

2. cow   pig   chicken   tiger

   _____

3. cub   camel   kitten   joey

   _____

4. squirrel   honeybee   bat   bird

   _____

5. walrus   lion   penguin   seal

   _____

6. beetle   ladybug   cricket   spider

   _____

7. bear   shark   whale   octopus

   _____

B. Three of the animal names above are compound words.
   Write them on the lines.

   _____   _____   _____

Name: _____

At the Produce Stand

Write three words to describe how each vegetable looks, feels, and tastes.

carrot

looks _____

feels _____

tastes _____

celery

looks _____

feels _____

tastes _____

corn

looks _____

feels _____

tastes _____

potato

looks _____

feels _____

tastes _____

onion

looks _____

feels _____

tastes _____

peas

looks _____

feels _____

tastes _____

Vocabulary Fundamentals • EMC 2802 • © Evan-Moor Corp.

Name: _____

Beach Day

There is a lot happening at the beach!
Circle the actions that you see. Write the **–ing** words on the lines below.

1. _____   5. _____   9. _____

2. _____   6. _____   10. _____

3. _____   7. _____   11. _____

4. _____   8. _____   12. _____

Name: _____

House and Home

Use the clues to find compound words that contain
the word **house** or **home**.

1. when you go away and
   miss your family   home____ ____ ____ ____

2. school papers you take home   home____ ____ ____ ____

3. a person you invite to spend the night   house____ ____ ____ ____ ____

4. food that is not store-bought   home____ ____ ____ ____

5. where Rover sleeps   ____ ____ ____house

6. indoor greenery   house____ ____ ____ ____ ____

7. where birds live   ____ ____ ____ ____house

8. a place to grow plants   ____ ____ ____ ____ ____house

9. where firefighters sleep   ____ ____ ____ ____house

10. the place you come from   home____ ____ ____ ____

11. an insect pest   house____ ____ ____

12. a small house for a toy   ____ ____ ____ ____house

13. a person paid to clean   house____ ____ ____ ____ ____ ____

14. gives warning to ships   ____ ____ ____ ____ ____house

            Vocabulary Fundamentals • EMC 2802 • © Evan-Moor Corp.

Mitten Matchup

Find pairs of antonyms. Color the two mittens in each pair the same color.
There are eight pairs, so you will need eight different colors.

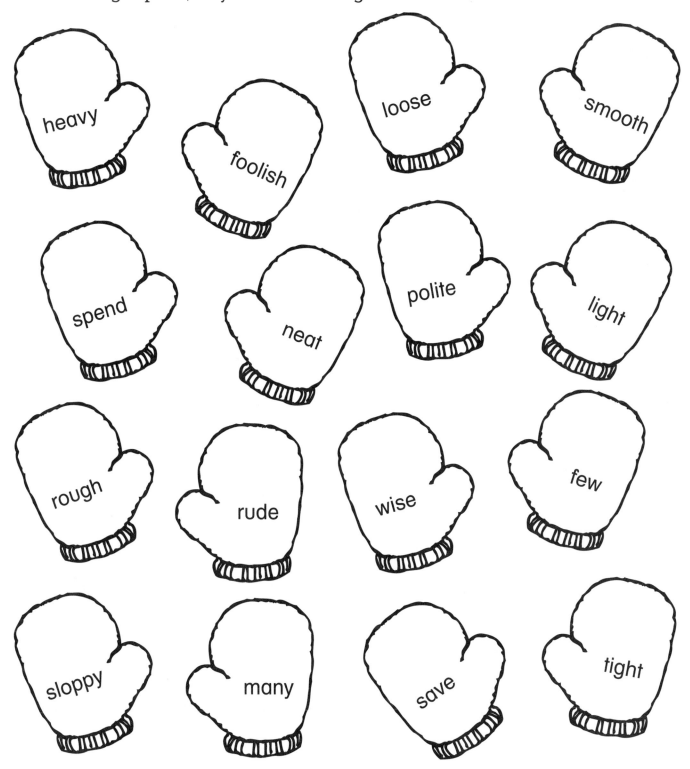

heavy

foolish

loose

smooth

spend

neat

polite

light

rough

rude

wise

few

sloppy

many

save

tight

Twos and Threes

Some things just go together.
Fill in the blanks to complete each pair or trio.

1. salt and _____

2. shoes and _____

3. lock and _____

4. ketchup and _____

5. peanut butter and _____

6. macaroni and _____

7. thunder and _____

8. knife, fork, and _____

9. red, white, and _____

10. morning, noon, and _____

11. bacon, lettuce, and _____

12. stop, drop, and _____

13. rock, paper, _____

14. ready, set, _____

15. Wynken, Blynken, and _____

   Vocabulary Fundamentals • EMC 2802 • © Evan-Moor Corp.

Name: _____

Trees

These names of trees are missing some letters.
Use the letters in the box to fill in the blanks. You may use
each letter only once. Cross off the letters as you use them.

a c d e e f h i i k l l l m m o p p p r r u w

1. e _____ m

2. _____ i r

3. o a _____

4. p _____ n e

5. p a l _____

6. _____ e a r

7. a p p _____ e

8. _____ _____ e r r y

9. c e d a _____

10. b _____ r c h

11. s _____ r u c e

12. w i l l _____ _____

13. c h _____ s t n _____ t

14. _____ e d w o o _____

Write the letters from the box that are left over: _____ _____ _____ _____ _____

Unscramble the letters to name another tree: _____

Circle the food that comes from this tree.

Name: _____

Flower Power

Some words have many synonyms.
Fill in each flower petal with a synonym for the word
in the center of the flower.

Name: _____

Body Parts

Sometimes, words that are used to name body parts are also used to describe other things. For example, the mouth of a jar is the part where it opens and, just like you, an apple has a skin.

Use the words in the box to label the pictures.

legs	teeth	ear	heel	hands
neck	arms	eyes	head	

Animal Rhyme Time

Use the clues to find the two-word rhyming answers.
Examples: chubby kitty = fat cat
          large hog = big pig

1. amusing rabbit   _____ _____

2. pleasant rodents   _____ _____

3. dessert for a reptile _____ _____

4. two grizzlies   _____ _____

5. carpet made from insects _____ _____

6. wet puppy   _____ _____

7. hot drink for a honey-maker _____ _____

8. cozy insect   _____ _____

9. poky black bird   _____ _____

10. chicken yard   _____ _____

11. unwell bird   _____ _____

12. bath for a baby bear _____ _____

Vocabulary Fundamentals • EMC 2802 • © Evan-Moor Corp.

ANSWER KEY

Page 6

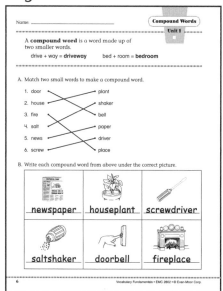

Page 7

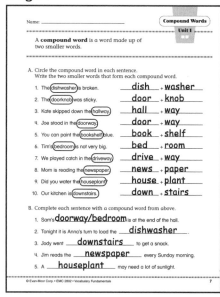

Page 8

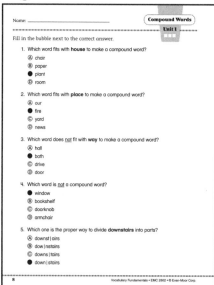

Page 9

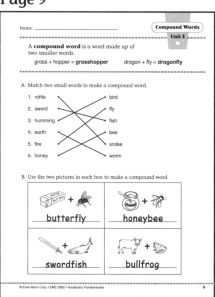

Page 10

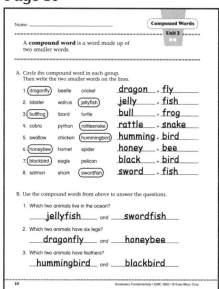

Page 11

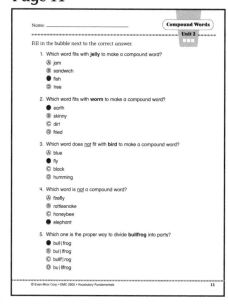

Page 12

Name: _____

Compound Words
Unit 3

A **compound word** is a word made up of two smaller words.

note + book = **notebook**　　lunch + box = **lunchbox**

A. Circle the compound word in each sentence.

1. The (playground) at my school has a big slide.
2. I am learning to type on the (keyboard).
3. Maria's (classroom) is at the end of the hall.
4. Andy does his (homework) at the table.
5. It is a good idea to (proofread) your work.

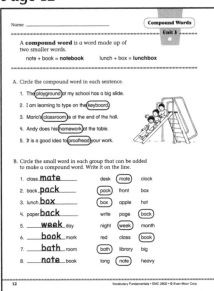

B. Circle the small word in each group that can be added to make a compound word. Write it on the line.

1. class **mate** — desk (mate) clock
2. back **pack** — (pack) front box
3. lunch **box** — (box) apple hot
4. paper **back** — write page (back)
5. **week** day — night (week) month
6. **book** mark — red class (book)
7. **bath** room — (bath) library big
8. **note** book — long (note) heavy

12　Vocabulary Fundamentals • EMC 2802 • © Evan-Moor Corp.

Page 13

Name: _____

Compound Words
Unit 3

A **compound word** is a word made up of two smaller words.

A. Choose a compound word from the box to answer each clue.

| notebook | backpack | keyboard |
| weekday | playground | proofread |

1. where you go at recess — **playground**
2. a bag to carry your books — **backpack**
3. what you type on at the computer — **keyboard**
4. not Saturday or Sunday — **weekday**
5. to check your work for mistakes — **proofread**
6. store your papers in this — **notebook**

B. Use the small words in the box to make two compound words. Then use each new word in a sentence.

| lunch | work | home | box |

Compound words: **lunchbox** and **homework**

1. **Sentences will vary.** _____
_____
2. _____
_____

© Evan-Moor Corp. • EMC 2802 • Vocabulary Fundamentals　13

Page 14

Name: _____

Compound Words
Unit 3

A **compound word** is a word made up of two smaller words.

Choose the best word for each blank.

| proofread | classroom | homework | bookmark |
| paperback | backpack | classmate | playground |

I got to school early today. I went out to the **playground** to swing on the bars. I saw my **classmate** Anna on my way there. She was sitting under a tree, reading a **paperback** book. When she saw me, she asked me to sit with her. She put a **bookmark** in her book so she would not lose her place.

We talked about the spelling **homework** that the teacher had given us yesterday. I thought it was hard, but Anna said it was easy for her. She offered to **proofread** my work. I got my spelling paper out of my **backpack** and gave it to Anna. She looked it over and found a mistake. Luckily, I had a pencil so I could fix it. Then the bell rang and we raced to our **classroom**.

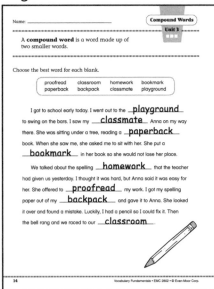

14　Vocabulary Fundamentals • EMC 2802 • © Evan-Moor Corp.

Page 15

Name: _____

Synonyms
Unit 1

Synonyms are words that have almost the same meaning.

Silent is a synonym for **quiet**.
Soar is a synonym for **fly**.

A. Choose a synonym from the box to replace each word under the line.

| Perhaps | simple | silent | soar |

1. All of the students were **silent** during the test.
　　　　　　　　　　　　　(quiet)
2. Lucy watched the eagle **soar** through the air.
　　　　　　　　　　　　　(fly)
3. Dad said, "**Perhaps** we will go to the movies tonight."
　　　　　　　(Maybe)
4. Tara thought the math problem was too **simple**.
　　　　　　　　　　　　　　　　　　(easy)

B. Circle the two synonyms in each sentence.

1. (Perhaps) it will rain, and (maybe) there will be thunder.
2. It was (easy) for Jacob to learn to play the (simple) game.
3. It would be fun to (fly) like a bird and (soar) through the air!
4. The students grew (quiet) when the teacher asked them to be (silent).

© Evan-Moor Corp. • EMC 2802 • Vocabulary Fundamentals　15

Page 16

Name: _____

Synonyms
Unit 1

Synonyms are words that have almost the same meaning.

A. Choose the correct word for each blank.

| perhaps | simple | silent | soar |

1. If you are quiet, you may be **silent**.
2. If a job is easy, it is **simple**.
3. Another word for maybe is **perhaps**.
4. When you fly, you **soar** through the air.

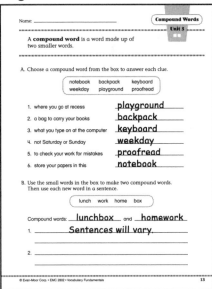

B. Use a synonym from above to write a sentence for each bold word.

Sentences will vary but must include:

1. Write a sentence using a synonym for **fly**.
_____ **soar** _____

2. Write a sentence using a synonym for **simple**.
_____ **easy** _____

3. Write a sentence using a synonym for **quiet**.
_____ **silent** _____

16　Vocabulary Fundamentals • EMC 2802 • © Evan-Moor Corp.

Page 17

Name: _____

Synonyms
Unit 1

Synonyms are words that have almost the same meaning.

Fill in each blank with the best synonym from the box.

| quiet | fly | easy | maybe |
| silent | soar | simple | perhaps |

Early this morning, my brother Anthony and I went to the park to **fly** our new kite. We were **silent/quiet** as we tiptoed out the door. Once we got to the park, we took out the kite. The kite had several pieces, but it was still **easy** for me to put it together. **Perhaps/Maybe** it would have been harder if my brother hadn't helped me.

When we got to the park, it was very **quiet/silent**. I could not hear the wind at all. I worried that **maybe/perhaps** there was not enough wind to fly the kite. We tried anyway. I held the string, and my brother threw the kite into the air. It went up and up! We watched it **soar** high in the sky. Then I tried a few **simple** tricks. I made the kite dive and spin.

Soon, it was time to go. We wanted to get home for breakfast. Dad was making chocolate chip pancakes!

© Evan-Moor Corp. • EMC 2802 • Vocabulary Fundamentals　17

Page 18

Name: _____

Synonyms
Unit 2

Synonyms are words that have almost the same meaning.

Think is a synonym for **believe**.
Strong is a synonym for **powerful**.

A. Choose a synonym from the box to replace each word under the line.

| powerful | believe | glossy | exit |

1. We will **exit** when the movie is over.
　　　　　　(leave)
2. I **believe** it is your turn to do the dishes tonight.
　　　(think)
3. The **powerful** man lifted the heavy rock.
　　　　　(strong)
4. Hannah's new plastic purse is bright and **glossy**.
　　　　　　　　　　　　　　　　　　(shiny)

B. Fill in each blank with a word from the box.

1. **Leave** is a synonym for **exit**.
2. **Think** is a synonym for **believe**.
3. **Shiny** is a synonym for **glossy**.
4. **Strong** is a synonym for **powerful**.

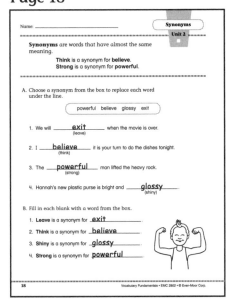

18　Vocabulary Fundamentals • EMC 2802 • © Evan-Moor Corp.

Page 19

Name: _____

Synonyms
Unit 2

Synonyms are words that have almost the same meaning.

A. Draw lines to match the synonyms.

1. exit — shiny
2. believe — leave
3. glossy — strong
4. powerful — think

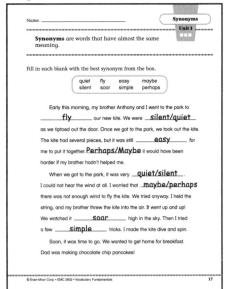

B. Use a synonym from above to write a sentence for each bold word.

Sentences will vary but must include:

1. Write a sentence using a synonym for **think**.
_____ **believe** _____

2. Write a sentence using a synonym for **strong**.
_____ **powerful** _____

3. Write a sentence using a synonym for **shiny**.
_____ **glossy** _____

4. Write a sentence using a synonym for **leave**.
_____ **exit** _____

© Evan-Moor Corp. • EMC 2802 • Vocabulary Fundamentals　19

Page 20

Name: _____

Synonyms
Unit 2

Fill in the bubble next to the correct answer.

1. Synonyms are words that _____.
　Ⓐ have opposite meanings
　● have almost the same meaning
　Ⓒ sound the same but have different meanings
　Ⓓ are made from two smaller words

2. Which word is a synonym for **leave**?
　Ⓐ tree
　Ⓑ come
　Ⓒ enter
　● exit

3. Which word is a synonym for **powerful**?
　Ⓐ large
　Ⓑ brave
　● strong
　Ⓓ weak

4. Which two words are synonyms?
　● shiny, glossy
　Ⓑ shiny, tiny
　Ⓒ slippery, glossy
　Ⓓ shiny, smooth

5. Which sentence contains a synonym for **think**?
　Ⓐ I know it will rain today.
　Ⓑ I hope it will rain today.
　● I believe it will rain today.
　Ⓓ I want it to rain today.

20　Vocabulary Fundamentals • EMC 2802 • © Evan-Moor Corp.

Page 21

Name: _____

Synonyms
Unit 3

Synonyms are words that have almost the same meaning.

Certain is a synonym for **sure**.
Weep is a synonym for **cry**.

A. Complete each sentence with a synonym from the box.

certain   weep   delete   nearly

1. The sad movie made Mara **weep** (cry)

2. Colin wanted to **delete** (erase) a misspelled word.

3. Tony was **certain** (sure) he had shut the door.

4. Jade had **nearly** (almost) enough money for a train ticket.

B. Circle the two synonyms in each sentence.

1. Nathan is (nearly) four feet tall and weighs (almost) eighty pounds.
2. Sarah started to (weep) when she saw her little sister (cry).
3. Sam wasn't (sure) he knew the way, but I was (certain) that I did.

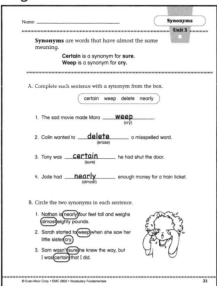

© Evan-Moor Corp. • EMC 2802 • Vocabulary Fundamentals   21

Page 22

Name: _____

Synonyms
Unit 3

Synonyms are words that have almost the same meaning.

Rewrite each sentence. Use a synonym from the box in place of the underlined word.

weep   delete   nearly   certain

Sentences will vary but must include:

1. Tara knew it was almost time to leave for school.
   nearly

2. Ben began to cry when he could not find his dog.
   weep

3. Lily knew she should erase her last sentence.
   delete

4. David was sure he would win the race.
   certain

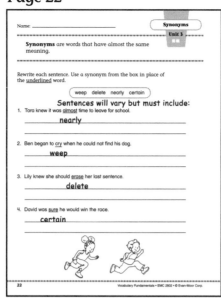

22   Vocabulary Fundamentals • EMC 2802 • © Evan-Moor Corp.

Page 23

Name: _____

Synonyms
Unit 3

Fill in the bubble next to the correct answer.

1. Which word is a synonym for **nearly**?
   Ⓐ dearly
   Ⓑ always
   ● almost
   Ⓓ never

2. Which sentence contains a synonym for **delete**?
   Ⓐ I will write the word.
   ● I will erase the word.
   Ⓒ I will read the word.
   Ⓓ I will type the word.

3. Which sentence contains a synonym for **cry**?
   ● The little girl began to weep when her mother left.
   Ⓑ The little girl began to laugh when her mother left.
   Ⓒ The little girl began to yell when her mother left.
   Ⓓ The little girl began to talk when her mother left.

4. Which two words are synonyms?
   Ⓐ sure, unsure
   Ⓑ maybe, certain
   Ⓒ sure, possibly
   ● sure, certain

5. Which two words are synonyms?
   Ⓐ erase, invisible
   Ⓑ weep, wept
   Ⓒ nearly, almost
   Ⓓ almost, certain

© Evan-Moor Corp. • EMC 2802 • Vocabulary Fundamentals   23

Page 24

Name: _____

Synonyms
Unit 4

Synonyms are words that have almost the same meaning.

Far is a synonym for **distant**.
Afraid is a synonym for **fearful**.

A. Write a synonym from the box for the underlined word in each sentence.

discover   vacant   fearful   distant

1. If the dark makes you feel afraid, you are **fearful**
2. A tree that is far away from you is **distant**
3. If you find a trail in the woods, you **discover** it.
4. An empty house that no one lives in is **vacant**

B. Circle the synonym for the bold word in each row.

1. **find**   lose   (discover)   search
2. **afraid** (fearful)   brave   shy
3. **empty**   alone   full   (vacant)
4. **far**   away   (distant)   close

C. Circle the synonyms for **fearful** and **discover** in this sentence.
I was (afraid) I would not (find) my pencil before the spelling test!

24   Vocabulary Fundamentals • EMC 2802 • © Evan-Moor Corp.

Page 25

Name: _____

Synonyms
Unit 4

Synonyms are words that have almost the same meaning.

Use a synonym from the box to write a sentence for each bold word. Underline the synonym.

distant   vacant   fearful   discover

Sentences will vary but must include:

1. Write a sentence using a synonym for **find**.
   discover

2. Write a sentence using a synonym for **empty**.
   vacant

3. Write a sentence using a synonym for **far**.
   distant

4. Write a sentence using a synonym for **afraid**.
   fearful

© Evan-Moor Corp. • EMC 2802 • Vocabulary Fundamentals   25

Page 26

Name: _____

Synonyms
Unit 4

Synonyms are words that have almost the same meaning.

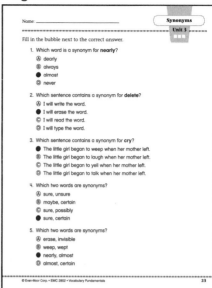

Fill in each blank with the best synonym from the box.

afraid   find   far   empty
fearful   discover   distant   vacant

Tim and his sister Julie wandered away from the campground. Before long, they were lost. It was getting dark, and they both felt **afraid**. Julie looked around. Far away through the trees, she could see a **distant** cabin. When they got to the cabin, Tim peeked through a window. There were no people inside. The cabin was **vacant**.

The door was not locked, so they went inside. Tim tried to **find** something to eat, but there was no food. The cabinets were all **empty**. Then Julie heard something outside. Someone was calling her name! Tim and Julie ran outside to **discover** that their parents had found them.

"Thank goodness you are okay," said their mother. "We were so **fearful** when you did not come back."

"You must not go so **far** from camp," said their father. Tim and Julie knew he was right.

26   Vocabulary Fundamentals • EMC 2802 • © Evan-Moor Corp.

Page 27

Name: _____

Synonyms
Unit 5

Synonyms are words that have almost the same meaning. A word may have more than one synonym.

Snooze and **rest** are synonyms for **nap**.
Chuckle and **giggle** are synonyms for **laugh**.

A. Complete each sentence with a synonym from the box.

chuckle   reply   peek   rest

1. Another word for **answer** is **reply**
2. Another word for **nap** is **rest**
3. Another word for **look** is **peek**
4. Another word for **laugh** is **chuckle**

B. Complete each sentence with a synonym from the box.

giggle   respond   peer   snooze

1. If you take a **nap**, you are having a **snooze**
2. If you **answer** someone, you **respond** to her.
3. When you **laugh** at a funny TV show, you **giggle**
4. When you **look** at your friend, you **peer** at him.

© Evan-Moor Corp. • EMC 2802 • Vocabulary Fundamentals   27

Page 28

Name: _____

Synonyms
Unit 5

Synonyms are words that have almost the same meaning.

Choose a synonym from the box to replace the word under the line.

rest   chuckle   reply   peer
respond   snooze   peek   giggle

1. The little girl began to **giggle** (laugh) at the clown.
   The funny joke made Grandpa **chuckle** (laugh)

2. Drew lay down to **rest** (sleep) after the big game.
   Dad wanted to **snooze** (sleep) on the couch.

3. Karen wrote a **reply** (answer) to the e-mail.
   Tom knew he had to **respond** (answer) truthfully.

4. Cassie took a quick **peek** (look) at the birthday cake.
   Mario wanted to **peer** (look) through the telescope.

28   Vocabulary Fundamentals • EMC 2802 • © Evan-Moor Corp.

Page 29

Name: _____

Synonyms
Unit 5

Fill in the bubble next to the correct answer.

1. Which word does not tell what a person would do after hearing a joke?
   Ⓐ giggle
   Ⓑ laugh
   Ⓒ chuckle
   ● sleep

2. Which word does not tell what a person would do if he were tired?
   Ⓐ rest
   ● shout
   Ⓒ sleep
   Ⓓ snooze

3. Which two words are synonyms for **answer**?
   Ⓐ reply, ask
   Ⓑ reply, speak
   ● reply, respond
   Ⓓ ask, respond

4. Which two words are synonyms for **look**?
   Ⓐ peer, eye
   ● peer, peek
   Ⓒ know, peek
   Ⓓ peer, peel

5. Which sentence contains synonyms for **answer** and **laugh**?
   ● The teacher's reply made the class giggle.
   Ⓑ The teacher's reply made the class cry.
   Ⓒ The teacher's question made the class giggle.
   Ⓓ The teacher's question made the class think.

© Evan-Moor Corp. • EMC 2802 • Vocabulary Fundamentals   29

© Evan-Moor Corp. • EMC 2802 • Vocabulary Fundamentals

155

Page 30

Synonyms
Unit 6

Synonyms are words that have almost the same meaning. A word may have more than one synonym.
Repair and **mend** are synonyms for **fix**.
Toss and **pitch** are synonyms for **throw**.

A. Match each sentence to a synonym for the underlined word.
1. Can you gently throw the ball to me? — repair
2. We need to fix our car before our trip. — hurt
3. Be very careful not to harm the baby. — piece
4. The model plane was missing a part. — toss

B. Match each sentence to a synonym for the underlined word.
1. The puppy might harm the new carpet. — section
2. The ending was the best part of the book. — pitch
3. Can you please fix my broken doll? — damage
4. I can throw the ball across the field! — mend

C. Fill in each blank with an underlined word from above.
1. If you repair something, you _____fix_____ it.
2. When you toss a ball, you _____throw_____ it.
3. If you eat a piece of cake, you eat a _____part_____ of the cake.

Page 31

Synonyms
Unit 6

Synonyms are words that have almost the same meaning. A word may have more than one synonym.

A. Circle two synonyms for the bold word in each row.
1. **fix** (repair) try (mend) break
2. **throw** catch (toss) (pitch) hit
3. **part** comb cart (piece) (section)
4. **hurt** (harm) stop have (damage)

B. Use a synonym you circled above to write a sentence for each bold word. Underline the synonym.
1. Write a sentence using a synonym for **throw**.
Sentences will vary but must include:
toss/pitch
_____

2. Write a sentence using a synonym for **hurt**.
harm/damage
_____

3. Write a sentence using a synonym for **part**.
piece/section
_____

Page 32

Synonyms
Unit 6

Synonyms are words that have almost the same meaning.

Fill in each blank with the best synonym from the box.

fix	part	hurt	toss
repair	piece	damage	throw

This morning, my brother Greg tried to _____throw/toss_____ a ball to me while I was riding my bike. I tried to catch the ball, but I crashed instead! It was scary, but I did not get _____hurt_____.

When I picked up my bike, I saw that one of the tires was flat. I would need help to _____repair/fix_____ it.

I asked my dad to help me. He looked at my bike and said that the tire would be easy to _____fix/repair_____. He took my bike to the _____part_____ of the garage where he keeps the tools. He showed me how to patch the tube inside the tire with a small _____piece_____ of rubber. Soon, my bike was as good as new!

Then Dad had a talk with us. Dad told us that it is not safe to _____toss/throw_____ a ball at someone who is riding a bike. I could have been hurt, and there could have been real _____damage_____ to the bike. We knew Dad was right. We won't do it again.

Page 33

Synonyms
Unit 7

Synonyms are words that have almost the same meaning. A word may have more than one synonym.
Damp and **moist** are synonyms for **wet**.
Skinny, slim, and **slender** are synonyms for **thin**.

A. Circle the synonym for **strange** in each sentence.
1. Sophie thought her grandma's big red hat was (odd).
2. It was (unusual) for Carl to skip dessert.

B. Circle the synonym for **wet** in each sentence.
1. My shirt was (damp) with sweat after the soccer game.
2. Dad said to get the sponge (moist) before wiping the table.

C. Circle the synonym for **surprised** in each sentence.
1. The magic show (amazed) everyone who saw it.
2. Jim was (astonished) to find a new bike in the driveway!

D. Circle the synonym for **skinny** in each sentence.
1. The lost puppy was (thin) and hungry when we found her.
2. The (slender) snake was wrapped around a branch.
3. The flower had a (slim) stem and sharp thorns!

Page 34

Synonyms
Unit 7

Synonyms are words that have almost the same meaning. A word may have more than one synonym.

Use a synonym from the box to write a sentence for each bold word. Underline the synonym.

| unusual | moist | astonished | thin |

Sentences will vary but must include:
1. Write a sentence using a synonym for **wet**.
moist
_____

2. Write a sentence using a synonym for **skinny**.
thin
_____

3. Write a sentence using a synonym for **strange**.
unusual
_____

4. Write a sentence using a synonym for **surprised**.
astonished
_____

Page 35

Synonyms
Unit 7

Fill in the bubble next to the correct answer.
1. Which word is not a synonym for **thin**?
Ⓐ slender
Ⓑ slim
● little
Ⓓ skinny

2. Which two words are synonyms for **strange**?
● odd, unusual
Ⓑ usual, unusual
Ⓒ odd, normal
Ⓓ odd, old

3. Which two words are synonyms for **wet**?
Ⓐ damp, cold
Ⓑ warm, dry
● moist, damp
Ⓓ moist, dry

4. Which sentence contains synonyms for **amazed** and **odd**?
Ⓐ We were surprised by her new hairstyle.
Ⓑ We were upset by her unusual hairstyle.
Ⓒ We were surprised by her adorable hairstyle.
● We were surprised by her unusual hairstyle.

5. Which sentence contains synonyms for **slender** and **damp**?
Ⓐ My dog looks unusual when he is moist.
Ⓑ My dog looks thin when he is tired.
● My dog looks skinny when he is wet.
Ⓓ My dog looks odd when he is moist.

Page 36

Precise Language
Unit 1

Use exact words to make your meaning clear.
words for eat: bite, chew, munch, gobble, nibble, chomp, dine
words for drink: sip, slurp, gulp, lap

A. Circle the word that makes the meaning clear.

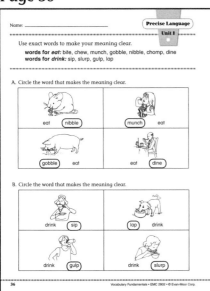

eat (nibble)   (munch) eat
(gobble) eat   eat (dine)

B. Circle the word that makes the meaning clear.

drink (sip)   (lap) drink
drink (gulp)   drink (slurp)

Page 37

Precise Language
Unit 1

Use exact words to make your meaning clear.
words for eat: bite, chew, munch, gobble, nibble, chomp, dine
words for drink: sip, slurp, gulp, lap

Complete each sentence with a word for **eat** or **drink**. Choose the word from above that gives the clearest meaning.

1. You make a lot of noise if you _____slurp_____ your soup.
(drink)
2. Don't _____chomp/munch_____ carrot sticks during a movie!
(eat)
3. My hamster likes to take his time and _____nibble_____ his food.
(eat)
4. When I _____gulp_____ soda quickly, I feel sick.
(drink)
5. On my birthday, the whole family will _____dine_____ at a restaurant.
(eat)
6. The dog will _____chew_____ her bone and _____lap_____ water.
(eat)   (drink)
7. My grandmother likes to chat with her friends while they _____sip_____ tea.
(drink)
8. If you are hungry, _____munch/chomp_____ on an apple.
(eat)

Page 38

Precise Language
Unit 1

Use exact words to make your meaning clear.
words for eat: bite, chew, munch, gobble, nibble, chomp, dine
words for drink: sip, slurp, gulp, lap

Fill in each blank with a word for **eat** or **drink**. Choose the word from above that gives the clearest meaning.

Grandpa Gus picked me up at 1:00 to go to the zoo. I was late, so I had to _____gobble_____ down my lunch. Grandpa brought bottles of lemonade for us to _____sip_____ in the car. I still had a lot of lemonade left when we parked the car, so I had to _____slurp/gulp_____ it down.

We got to the zoo at feeding time. We found out that each animal eats its food in its own way. Giraffes _____chew/munch/nibble_____ on tiny leaves. Lions _____chomp/chew_____ hungrily on meat and bones. Zebras _____munch/chew_____ on grass and hay.

Watching the animals eat made Grandpa and me hungry. We were in luck! A sign at the zoo restaurant said, "Kids under 12 _____dine_____ free." I couldn't wait to _____bite_____ into a hot dog!

Page 39

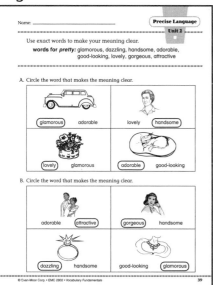

Precise Language — Unit 2

Use exact words to make your meaning clear.
words for *pretty*: glamorous, dazzling, handsome, adorable, good-looking, lovely, gorgeous, attractive

A. Circle the word that makes the meaning clear.

- (glamorous) adorable
- lovely (handsome)
- (lovely) glamorous
- (adorable) good-looking

B. Circle the word that makes the meaning clear.

- adorable (attractive)
- (gorgeous) handsome
- (dazzling) handsome
- good-looking (glamorous)

© Evan-Moor Corp. • EMC 2802 • Vocabulary Fundamentals   39

Page 40

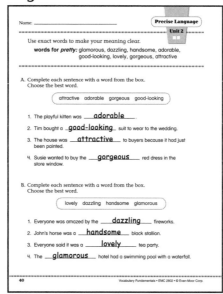

Name: _____

Precise Language — Unit 2

Use exact words to make your meaning clear.
words for *pretty*: glamorous, dazzling, handsome, adorable, good-looking, lovely, gorgeous, attractive

A. Complete each sentence with a word from the box. Choose the best word.

    attractive adorable gorgeous good-looking

1. The playful kitten was **adorable**.
2. Tim bought a **good-looking** suit to wear to the wedding.
3. The house was **attractive** to buyers because it had just been painted.
4. Susie wanted to buy the **gorgeous** red dress in the store window.

B. Complete each sentence with a word from the box. Choose the best word.

    lovely dazzling handsome glamorous

1. Everyone was amazed by the **dazzling** fireworks.
2. John's horse was a **handsome** black stallion.
3. Everyone said it was a **lovely** tea party.
4. The **glamorous** hotel had a swimming pool with a waterfall.

40   Vocabulary Fundamentals • EMC 2802 • © Evan-Moor Corp.

Page 41

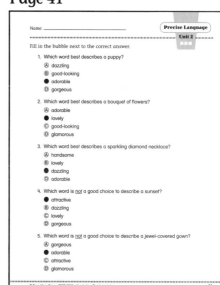

Name: _____

Precise Language — Unit 2

Fill in the bubble next to the correct answer.

1. Which word best describes a puppy?
   - Ⓐ dazzling
   - Ⓑ good-looking
   - ● adorable
   - Ⓓ gorgeous

2. Which word best describes a bouquet of flowers?
   - Ⓐ adorable
   - ● lovely
   - Ⓒ good-looking
   - Ⓓ glamorous

3. Which word best describes a sparkling diamond necklace?
   - Ⓐ handsome
   - Ⓑ lovely
   - ● dazzling
   - Ⓓ adorable

4. Which word is *not* a good choice to describe a sunset?
   - ● attractive
   - Ⓑ dazzling
   - Ⓒ lovely
   - Ⓓ gorgeous

5. Which word is *not* a good choice to describe a jewel-covered gown?
   - Ⓐ gorgeous
   - ● adorable
   - Ⓒ attractive
   - Ⓓ glamorous

© Evan-Moor Corp. • EMC 2802 • Vocabulary Fundamentals   41

Page 42

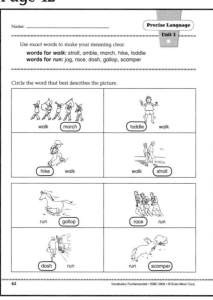

Name: _____

Precise Language — Unit 3

Use exact words to make your meaning clear.
words for *walk*: stroll, amble, march, hike, toddle
words for *run*: jog, race, dash, gallop, scamper

Circle the word that best describes the picture.

- walk (march)
- (toddle) walk
- (hike) walk
- walk (stroll)
- run (gallop)
- (race) run
- (dash) run
- run (scamper)

42   Vocabulary Fundamentals • EMC 2802 • © Evan-Moor Corp.

Page 43

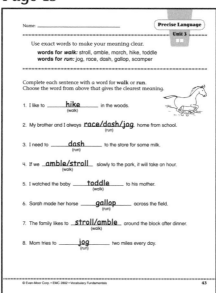

Name: _____

Precise Language — Unit 3

Use exact words to make your meaning clear.
words for *walk*: stroll, amble, march, hike, toddle
words for *run*: jog, race, dash, gallop, scamper

Complete each sentence with a word for **walk** or **run**.
Choose the word from above that gives the clearest meaning.

1. I like to **hike** _(walk)_ in the woods.
2. My brother and I always **race/dash/jog** _(run)_ home from school.
3. I need to **dash** _(run)_ to the store for some milk.
4. If we **amble/stroll** _(walk)_ slowly to the park, it will take an hour.
5. I watched the baby **toddle** _(walk)_ to his mother.
6. Sarah made her horse **gallop** _(run)_ across the field.
7. The family likes to **stroll/amble** _(walk)_ around the block after dinner.
8. Mom tries to **jog** _(run)_ two miles every day.

© Evan-Moor Corp. • EMC 2802 • Vocabulary Fundamentals   43

Page 44

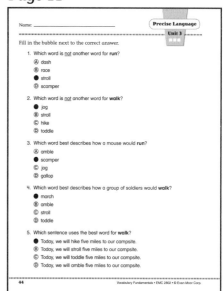

Name: _____

Precise Language — Unit 3

Fill in the bubble next to the correct answer.

1. Which word is *not* another word for **run**?
   - Ⓐ dash
   - Ⓑ race
   - ● stroll
   - Ⓓ scamper

2. Which word is *not* another word for **walk**?
   - ● jog
   - Ⓑ stroll
   - Ⓒ hike
   - Ⓓ toddle

3. Which word best describes how a mouse would **run**?
   - Ⓐ amble
   - ● scamper
   - Ⓒ jog
   - Ⓓ gallop

4. Which word best describes how a group of soldiers would **walk**?
   - ● march
   - Ⓑ amble
   - Ⓒ stroll
   - Ⓓ toddle

5. Which sentence uses the best word for **walk**?
   - ● Today, we will hike five miles to our campsite.
   - Ⓑ Today, we will stroll five miles to our campsite.
   - Ⓒ Today, we will toddle five miles to our campsite.
   - Ⓓ Today, we will amble five miles to our campsite.

44   Vocabulary Fundamentals • EMC 2802 • © Evan-Moor Corp.

Page 45

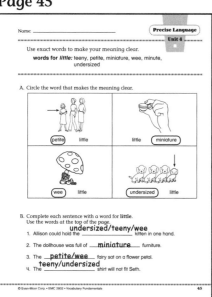

Name: _____

Precise Language — Unit 4

Use exact words to make your meaning clear.
words for *little*: teeny, petite, miniature, wee, minute, undersized

A. Circle the word that makes the meaning clear.

- (petite) little
- little (miniature)
- (wee) little
- (undersized) little

B. Complete each sentence with a word for **little**.
Use the words at the top of the page.

1. Allison could hold the **undersized/teeny/wee** kitten in one hand.
2. The dollhouse was full of **miniature** furniture.
3. The **petite/wee** fairy sat on a flower petal.
4. The **teeny/undersized** shirt will not fit Seth.

© Evan-Moor Corp. • EMC 2802 • Vocabulary Fundamentals   45

Page 46

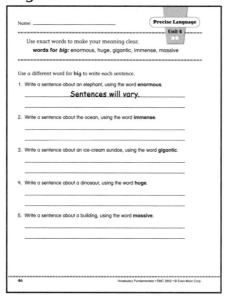

Name: _____

Precise Language — Unit 4

Use exact words to make your meaning clear.
words for *big*: enormous, huge, gigantic, immense, massive

Use a different word for **big** to write each sentence.

1. Write a sentence about an elephant, using the word **enormous**.
   Sentences will vary.
2. Write a sentence about the ocean, using the word **immense**.
3. Write a sentence about an ice-cream sundae, using the word **gigantic**.
4. Write a sentence about a dinosaur, using the word **huge**.
5. Write a sentence about a building, using the word **massive**.

46   Vocabulary Fundamentals • EMC 2802 • © Evan-Moor Corp.

Page 47

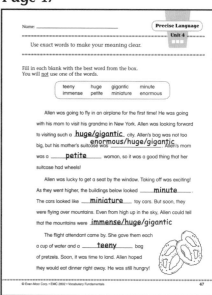

Name: _____

Precise Language — Unit 4

Use exact words to make your meaning clear.

Fill in each blank with the best word from the box.
You will *not* use one of the words.

    teeny   huge   gigantic   minute
    immense petite miniature   enormous

Allen was going to fly in an airplane for the first time! He was going with his mom to visit his grandma in New York. Allen was looking forward to visiting such a **huge/gigantic** city. Allen's bag was not too big, but his mother's suitcase was **enormous/huge/gigantic**. Allen's mom was a **petite** woman, so it was a good thing that her suitcase had wheels!

Allen was lucky to get a seat by the window. Taking off was exciting! As they went higher, the buildings below looked **minute**. The cars looked like **miniature** toy cars. But soon, they were flying over mountains. Even from high up in the sky, Allen could tell that the mountains were **immense/huge/gigantic**.

The flight attendant came by. She gave them each a cup of water and a **teeny** bag of pretzels. Soon, it was time to land. Allen hoped they would eat dinner right away. He was still hungry!

© Evan-Moor Corp. • EMC 2802 • Vocabulary Fundamentals   47

© Evan-Moor Corp. • EMC 2802 • Vocabulary Fundamentals   **157**

Page 48

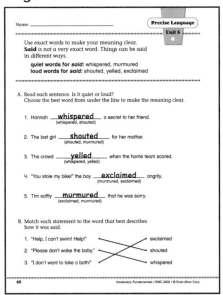

Precise Language
Unit 5

Use exact words to make your meaning clear.
Said is not a very exact word. Things can be said in different ways.

quiet words for **said**: whispered, murmured
loud words for **said**: shouted, yelled, exclaimed

A. Read each sentence. Is it quiet or loud?
Choose the best word from under the line to make the meaning clear.

1. Hannah **whispered** a secret to her friend.
   (whispered, shouted)

2. The lost girl **shouted** for her mother.
   (shouted, murmured)

3. The crowd **yelled** when the home team scored.
   (whispered, yelled)

4. "You stole my bike!" the boy **exclaimed** angrily.
   (murmured, exclaimed)

5. Tim softly **murmured** that he was sorry.
   (exclaimed, murmured)

B. Match each statement to the word that best describes how it was said.

1. "Help, I can't swim! Help!" — exclaimed
2. "Please don't wake the baby." — shouted
3. "I don't want to take a bath!" — whispered

(lines cross: 1 to shouted, 2 to whispered, 3 to exclaimed)

48   Vocabulary Fundamentals • EMC 2802 • © Evan-Moor Corp.

Page 49

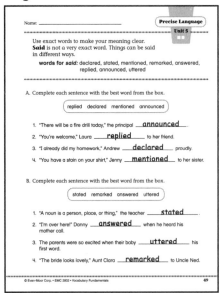

Name: _____

Precise Language
Unit 5

Use exact words to make your meaning clear.
Said is not a very exact word. Things can be said in different ways.

words for **said**: declared, stated, mentioned, remarked, answered, replied, announced, uttered

A. Complete each sentence with the best word from the box.

| replied declared mentioned announced |

1. "There will be a fire drill today," the principal **announced**.
2. "You're welcome," Laura **replied** to her friend.
3. "I already did my homework," Andrew **declared** proudly.
4. "You have a stain on your shirt," Jenny **mentioned** to her sister.

B. Complete each sentence with the best word from the box.

| stated remarked answered uttered |

1. "A noun is a person, place, or thing," the teacher **stated**.
2. "I'm over here!" Danny **answered** when he heard his mother call.
3. The parents were so excited when their baby **uttered** his first word.
4. "The bride looks lovely," Aunt Clara **remarked** to Uncle Ned.

© Evan-Moor Corp. • EMC 2802 • Vocabulary Fundamentals   49

Page 50

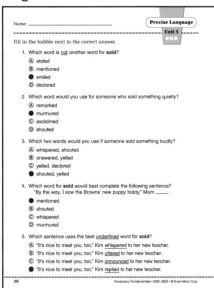

Name: _____

Precise Language
Unit 5

Fill in the bubble next to the correct answer.

1. Which word is _not_ another word for **said**?
   Ⓐ stated
   Ⓑ mentioned
   ● smiled
   Ⓓ declared

2. Which word would you use for someone who said something quietly?
   Ⓐ remarked
   ● murmured
   Ⓒ exclaimed
   Ⓓ shouted

3. Which two words would you use if someone said something loudly?
   Ⓐ whispered, shouted
   Ⓑ answered, yelled
   Ⓒ yelled, declared
   ● shouted, yelled

4. Which word for **said** would best complete the following sentence?
   "By the way, I saw the Browns' new puppy today," Mom _____.
   ● mentioned
   Ⓑ shouted
   Ⓒ whispered
   Ⓓ murmured

5. Which sentence uses the best _underlined_ word for **said**?
   Ⓐ "It's nice to meet you, too," Kim whispered to her new teacher.
   Ⓑ "It's nice to meet you, too," Kim uttered to her new teacher.
   Ⓒ "It's nice to meet you, too," Kim announced to her new teacher.
   ● "It's nice to meet you, too," Kim replied to her new teacher.

50   Vocabulary Fundamentals • EMC 2802 • © Evan-Moor Corp.

Page 51

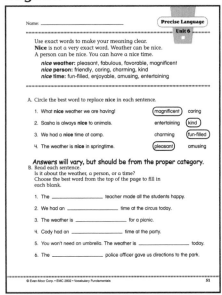

Name: _____

Precise Language
Unit 6

Use exact words to make your meaning clear.
Nice is not a very exact word. Weather can be nice.
A person can be nice. You can have a nice time.

nice **weather**: pleasant, fabulous, favorable, magnificent
nice **person**: friendly, caring, charming, kind
nice **time**: fun-filled, enjoyable, amusing, entertaining

A. Circle the best word to replace **nice** in each sentence.

1. What **nice** weather we are having! — (magnificent) / caring
2. Sasha is always **nice** to animals. — entertaining / (kind)
3. We had a **nice** time at camp. — charming / (fun-filled)
4. The weather is **nice** in springtime. — (pleasant) / amusing

Answers will vary, but should be from the proper category.
B. Read each sentence.
Is it about the weather, a person, or a time?
Choose the best word from the top of the page to fill in each blank.

1. The _____ teacher made all the students happy.
2. We had an _____ time at the circus today.
3. The weather is _____ for a picnic.
4. Cody had an _____ time at the party.
5. You won't need an umbrella. The weather is _____ today.
6. The _____ police officer gave us directions to the park.

© Evan-Moor Corp. • EMC 2802 • Vocabulary Fundamentals   51

Page 52

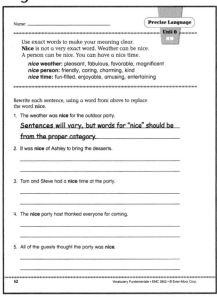

Name: _____

Precise Language
Unit 6

Use exact words to make your meaning clear.
Nice is not a very exact word. Weather can be nice.
A person can be nice. You can have a nice time.

nice **weather**: pleasant, fabulous, favorable, magnificent
nice **person**: friendly, caring, charming, kind
nice **time**: fun-filled, enjoyable, amusing, entertaining

Rewrite each sentence, using a word from above to replace the word **nice**.

1. The weather was **nice** for the outdoor party.
   Sentences will vary, but words for "nice" should be from the proper category.

2. It was **nice** of Ashley to bring the desserts.

3. Tom and Steve had a **nice** time at the party.

4. The **nice** party host thanked everyone for coming.

5. All of the guests thought the party was **nice**.

52   Vocabulary Fundamentals • EMC 2802 • © Evan-Moor Corp.

Page 53

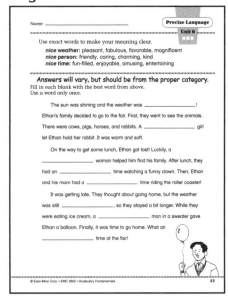

Name: _____

Precise Language
Unit 6

Use exact words to make your meaning clear.

nice **weather**: pleasant, fabulous, favorable, magnificent
nice **person**: friendly, caring, charming, kind
nice **time**: fun-filled, enjoyable, amusing, entertaining

Answers will vary, but should be from the proper category.
Fill in each blank with the best word from above.
Use a word only once.

The sun was shining and the weather was _____!

Ethan's family decided to go to the fair. First, they went to see the animals.
There were cows, pigs, horses, and rabbits. A _____ girl
let Ethan hold his rabbit. It was warm and soft.

On the way to get some lunch, Ethan got lost! Luckily, a
_____ woman helped him find his family. After lunch, they
had an _____ time watching a funny clown. Then, Ethan
and his mom had a _____ time riding the roller coaster!

It was getting late. They thought about going home, but the weather
was still _____, so they stayed a bit longer. While they
were eating ice cream, a _____ man in a sweater gave
Ethan a balloon. Finally, it was time to go home. What an
_____ time at the fair!

© Evan-Moor Corp. • EMC 2802 • Vocabulary Fundamentals   53

Page 54

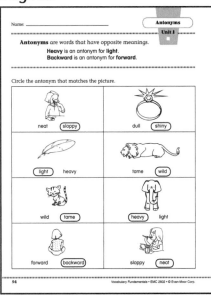

Name: _____

Antonyms
Unit 1

Antonyms are words that have opposite meanings.
Heavy is an antonym for **light**.
Backward is an antonym for **forward**.

Circle the antonym that matches the picture.

neat (sloppy)	dull (shiny)
(light) heavy	tame (wild)
wild (tame)	(heavy) light
forward (backward)	sloppy (neat)

54   Vocabulary Fundamentals • EMC 2802 • © Evan-Moor Corp.

Page 55

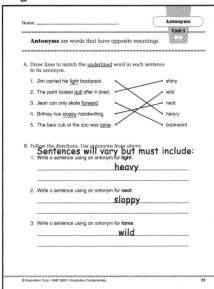

Name: _____

Antonyms
Unit 1

Antonyms are words that have opposite meanings.

A. Draw lines to match the _underlined_ word in each sentence to its antonym.

1. Jim carried his _light_ backpack. — shiny
2. The paint looked _dull_ after it dried. — wild
3. Jean can only skate _forward_. — neat
4. Britney has _sloppy_ handwriting. — heavy
5. The bear cub at the zoo was _tame_. — backward

B. Follow the directions. Use antonyms from above.
Sentences will vary but must include:
1. Write a sentence using an antonym for **light**.
   heavy

2. Write a sentence using an antonym for **neat**.
   sloppy

3. Write a sentence using an antonym for **tame**.
   wild

© Evan-Moor Corp. • EMC 2802 • Vocabulary Fundamentals   55

Page 56

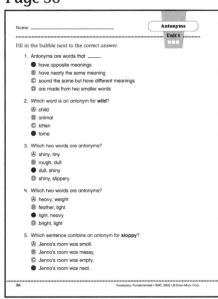

Name: _____

Antonyms
Unit 1

Fill in the bubble next to the correct answer.

1. Antonyms are words that _____.
   ● have opposite meanings
   Ⓑ have nearly the same meaning
   Ⓒ sound the same but have different meanings
   Ⓓ are made from two smaller words

2. Which word is an antonym for **wild**?
   Ⓐ child
   Ⓑ animal
   Ⓒ kitten
   ● tame

3. Which two words are antonyms?
   Ⓐ shiny, tiny
   Ⓑ rough, dull
   ● dull, shiny
   Ⓓ shiny, slippery

4. Which two words are antonyms?
   Ⓐ heavy, weight
   Ⓑ feather, light
   ● light, heavy
   Ⓓ bright, light

5. Which sentence contains an antonym for **sloppy**?
   Ⓐ Jenna's room was small.
   Ⓑ Jenna's room was messy.
   Ⓒ Jenna's room was empty.
   ● Jenna's room was neat.

56   Vocabulary Fundamentals • EMC 2802 • © Evan-Moor Corp.

Name: _____

Antonyms
Unit 2

Antonyms are words that have opposite meanings.
Above is an antonym for **below**.
Sharp is an antonym for **dull**.

A. Choose an antonym from the box to replace each word under the line.

rough   least   together   dull   above

1. The boys played __together__ at the playground.
   (apart)
2. We rode our bikes on the __rough__ road.
   (smooth)
3. Paul's pencil tip was __dull__.
   (sharp)
4. Jean keeps the plates __above__ the bowls.
   (below)
5. Kayla earned the __least__ amount of money.
   (most)

B. Fill in each blank with one of the words from the box.

1. **Apart** is an antonym for __together__
2. **Most** is an antonym for __least__
3. **Smooth** is an antonym for __rough__

© Evan-Moor Corp. • EMC 2802 • Vocabulary Fundamentals   57

Name: _____

Antonyms
Unit 2

Antonyms are words that have opposite meanings.

A. Circle the antonym for the bold word in each row.

1. **apart**   piece   above   (together)
2. **least**   (most)   more   less
3. **rough**   hard   (smooth)   shiny
4. **above**   (below)   over   around
5. **dull**   soft   afraid   (sharp)

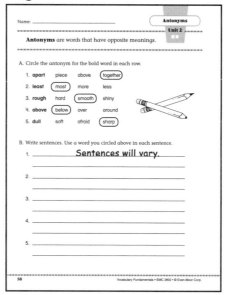

B. Write sentences. Use a word you circled above in each sentence.

1. _____ Sentences will vary. _____
2. _____
3. _____
4. _____
5. _____

58   Vocabulary Fundamentals • EMC 2802 • © Evan-Moor Corp.

Name: _____

Antonyms
Unit 2

Antonyms are words that have opposite meanings.

Fill in each blank with the best antonym from the box.

rough   apart   least   above
smooth   together   most   below

Jake and Cal are best friends. They spend __most__ of their time with each other. Yesterday, Jake and Cal went fishing __together__. When they got to the lake, the water was still and as __smooth__ as glass. They sat on the dock to fish. They sat __apart__ from each other so their fishing lines would not get tangled. They could see fish swimming in the water __below__ them. Soon, Jake had a bite! He reeled in his line until the fish was on the dock. The fish was silver with thick, __rough__ scales.

After a while, Cal looked at the sky __above__ them. He saw big, gray storm clouds. It was time to go home. This was the __least__ amount of fish they had ever caught, but they still had a great time together.

© Evan-Moor Corp. • EMC 2802 • Vocabulary Fundamentals   59

Name: _____

Antonyms
Unit 3

Antonyms are words that have opposite meanings.
Few is an antonym for **many**.
Always is an antonym for **never**.

A. Read each pair of sentences.
Circle the word that is an antonym for the underlined word.

1. Dad's car is <u>wide</u>. It was hard to drive it up the (narrow) driveway.
2. Andy wanted to <u>sell</u> his baseball cards. Derek wanted to (buy) them.
3. The forecaster said the rain would <u>increase</u> in the morning. Perhaps it will (decrease) by the afternoon.
4. Jody made (many) cookies. She gave her sister only a <u>few</u> of them.
5. Sharon (always) wore her boots when it rained. Her feet <u>never</u> got wet.

B. Use one of the underlined words above to complete each sentence.

1. **Buy** is an antonym for __sell__
2. **Many** is an antonym for __few__
3. **Narrow** is an antonym for __wide__
4. **Decrease** is an antonym for __increase__
5. **Always** is an antonym for __never__

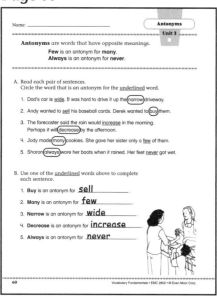

60   Vocabulary Fundamentals • EMC 2802 • © Evan-Moor Corp.

Name: _____

Antonyms
Unit 3

Antonyms are words that have opposite meanings.

A. Read each sentence.
Use an antonym from the box to write a sentence that has the opposite meaning.

never   many   narrow   buy   decrease

1. Carly wanted to <u>sell</u> cookies at the fair.
   Carly wanted to buy cookies at the fair.
2. Ben ate too <u>few</u> pancakes.
   Ben ate too many pancakes.
3. Kenny <u>always</u> combs his hair before school.
   Kenny never combs his hair before school.
4. The store plans to <u>increase</u> its prices.
   The store plans to decrease its prices.
5. Susie walked down the <u>wide</u> hallway.
   Susie walked down the narrow hallway.

B. Circle the antonym for the bold word in each row.

1. **decrease**   less   few   (increase)
2. **many**   (few)   more   some
3. **narrow**   thin   (wide)   fat

© Evan-Moor Corp. • EMC 2802 • Vocabulary Fundamentals   61

Name: _____

Antonyms
Unit 3

Fill in the bubble next to the correct answer.

1. Which word is an antonym for **increase**?
   ● decrease
   Ⓑ add
   Ⓒ into
   Ⓓ delight

2. Which sentence contains an antonym for **few**?
   Ⓐ John has more pennies.
   Ⓑ John has two pennies.
   ● John has many pennies.
   Ⓓ John has less pennies.

3. Which sentence contains an antonym for **never**?
   Ⓐ Chris rarely wears a hat.
   ● Chris always wears a hat.
   Ⓒ Chris usually wears a hat.
   Ⓓ Chris sometimes wears a hat.

4. Which two words are antonyms?
   Ⓐ buy, spend
   Ⓑ cell, sell
   ● buy, sell
   Ⓓ buy, store

5. Which two words are antonyms?
   Ⓐ narrow, skinny
   Ⓑ narrow, large
   Ⓒ across, wide
   ● narrow, wide

62   Vocabulary Fundamentals • EMC 2802 • © Evan-Moor Corp.

Name: _____

Antonyms
Unit 4

Antonyms are words that have opposite meanings.
Spend is an antonym for **save**.
Odd is an antonym for **even**.

A. Fill in the blank with the correct antonym.

1. Twenty-four is an __even__ number.
   (odd, even)
2. Jim's shoes were so __loose__ that they fell off his feet.
   (loose, tight)
3. Riding a bike without a helmet is a __foolish__ choice.
   (wise, foolish)
4. The __cool__ water felt good on the hot afternoon.
   (warm, cool)
5. Pedro wanted to __spend__ his money at the store.
   (spend, save)

B. Circle the antonyms in each sentence.

1. Mandy's shirt was (loose) but her sandals were (tight).
2. The (foolish) girl did not follow her friend's (wise) advice.
3. Jacob had to (save) his money for a long time before he could (spend) it on a bike.
4. We will solve the math problems with (odd) numbers and skip the problems with (even) numbers.

© Evan-Moor Corp. • EMC 2802 • Vocabulary Fundamentals   63

Name: _____

Antonyms
Unit 4

Antonyms are words that have opposite meanings.

A. Read each sentence.
Use an antonym from the box to write a sentence that has the opposite meaning.

warm   foolish   tight   spend

1. Tom wanted to <u>save</u> his money.
   Tom wanted to spend his money.
2. There was a <u>cool</u> breeze at the beach.
   There was a warm breeze at the beach.
3. Tad gave his little brother <u>wise</u> advice.
   Tad gave his little brother foolish advice.
4. Dad made a <u>loose</u> knot in the rope.
   Dad made a tight knot in the rope.

B. Use one of the underlined words above to complete each sentence.

1. **Warm** is an antonym for __cool__
2. **Tight** is an antonym for __loose__
3. **Spend** is an antonym for __save__
4. **Foolish** is an antonym for __wise__

64   Vocabulary Fundamentals • EMC 2802 • © Evan-Moor Corp.

Name: _____

Antonyms
Unit 4

Antonyms are words that have opposite meanings.

Fill in each blank with the best antonym from the box.

wise   tight   save   cool
foolish   loose   spend   warm

"Let's go to the beach!" exclaimed Dad. At first, Mom thought it was a __foolish__ idea because there were a lot of chores to do at home. Dad said that the weather was too __warm__ to do chores. Mom had to agree.

Lisa put on her swimsuit. She had grown since last summer and it was too __tight__! Luckily, her big sister Ann found one she had outgrown. Ann's old swimsuit was a little __loose__ on Lisa, but she could wear it.

At the beach, the girls went swimming in the __cool__ water. Then Mom gave them each some money to __spend__ on ice cream. Lisa wanted to __save__ her money, but the ice cream looked too good not to eat!

After ice cream, Mom said it would be __wise__ to wait a few minutes before going back into the water. The girls built a sand castle while waiting. Then they took one more swim before going home.

© Evan-Moor Corp. • EMC 2802 • Vocabulary Fundamentals   65

© Evan-Moor Corp. • EMC 2802 • Vocabulary Fundamentals

159

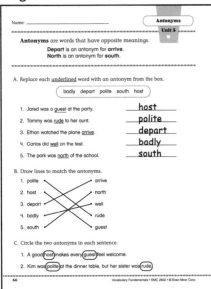

Name: _____

Antonyms
Unit 5

Antonyms are words that have opposite meanings.
Depart is an antonym for **arrive**.
North is an antonym for **south**.

A. Replace each underlined word with an antonym from the box.

| badly | depart | polite | south | host |

1. Jared was a guest at the party. **host**
2. Tammy was rude to her aunt. **polite**
3. Ethan watched the plane arrive. **depart**
4. Carlos did well on the test. **badly**
5. The park was north of the school. **south**

B. Draw lines to match the antonyms.

1. polite — arrive
2. host — north
3. depart — well
4. badly — rude
5. south — guest

C. Circle the two antonyms in each sentence.

1. A good host makes every guest feel welcome.
2. Kim was polite at the dinner table, but her sister was rude.

66 Vocabulary Fundamentals • EMC 2802 • © Evan-Moor Corp.

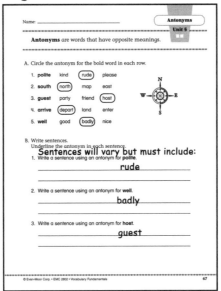

Name: _____

Antonyms
Unit 5

Antonyms are words that have opposite meanings.

A. Circle the antonym for the bold word in each row.

1. **polite**   kind   rude   please
2. **south**   north   map   east
3. **guest**   party   friend   host
4. **arrive**   depart   land   enter
5. **well**   good   badly   nice

B. Write sentences.
Underline the antonym in each sentence.

Sentences will vary but must include:
1. Write a sentence using an antonym for **polite**.
   rude
   _____
2. Write a sentence using an antonym for **well**.
   badly
   _____
3. Write a sentence using an antonym for **host**.
   guest
   _____

© Evan-Moor Corp. • EMC 2802 • Vocabulary Fundamentals 67

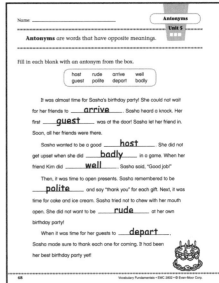

Name: _____

Antonyms
Unit 5

Antonyms are words that have opposite meanings.

Fill in each blank with an antonym from the box.

| host | rude | arrive | well |
| guest | polite | depart | badly |

It was almost time for Sasha's birthday party! She could not wait for her friends to **arrive**. Sasha heard a knock. Her first **guest** was at the door! Sasha let her friend in. Soon, all her friends were there.

Sasha wanted to be a good **host**. She did not get upset when she did **badly** in a game. When her friend Kim did **well**, Sasha said, "Good job!"

Then, it was time to open presents. Sasha remembered to be **polite** and say "thank you" for each gift. Next, it was time for cake and ice cream. Sasha tried not to chew with her mouth open. She did not want to be **rude** at her own birthday party!

When it was time for her guests to **depart**, Sasha made sure to thank each one for coming. It had been her best birthday party yet!

68 Vocabulary Fundamentals • EMC 2802 • © Evan-Moor Corp.

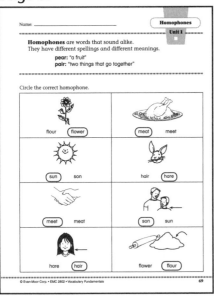

Name: _____

Homophones
Unit 1

Homophones are words that sound alike.
They have different spellings and different meanings.

pear: "a fruit"
pair: "two things that go together"

Circle the correct homophone.

flour (flower)	meat (meet)
(sun) son	hair (hare)
(meet) meat	(son) sun
hare (hair)	flower (flour)

© Evan-Moor Corp. • EMC 2802 • Vocabulary Fundamentals 69

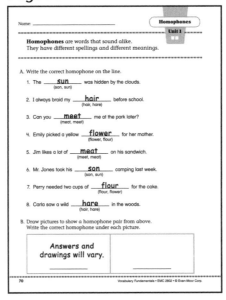

Name: _____

Homophones
Unit 1

Homophones are words that sound alike.
They have different spellings and different meanings.

A. Write the correct homophone on the line.

1. The **sun** was hidden by the clouds. (son, sun)
2. I always braid my **hair** before school. (hair, hare)
3. Can you **meet** me at the park later? (meat, meet)
4. Emily picked a yellow **flower** for her mother. (flower, flour)
5. Jim likes a lot of **meat** on his sandwich. (meet, meat)
6. Mr. Jones took his **son** camping last week. (son, sun)
7. Perry needed two cups of **flour** for the cake. (flour, flower)
8. Carla saw a wild **hare** in the woods. (hair, hare)

B. Draw pictures to show a homophone pair from above. Write the correct homophone under each picture.

Answers and drawings will vary.

70 Vocabulary Fundamentals • EMC 2802 • © Evan-Moor Corp.

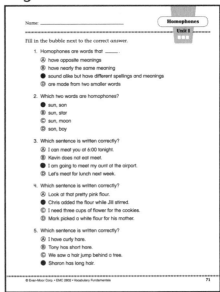

Name: _____

Homophones
Unit 1

Fill in the bubble next to the correct answer.

1. Homophones are words that _____.
   Ⓐ have opposite meanings
   Ⓑ have nearly the same meaning
   ● sound alike but have different spellings and meanings
   Ⓓ are made from two smaller words

2. Which two words are homophones?
   ● sun, son
   Ⓑ sun, star
   Ⓒ sun, moon
   Ⓓ son, boy

3. Which sentence is written correctly?
   Ⓐ I can meat you at 6:00 tonight.
   Ⓑ Kevin does not eat meet.
   ● I am going to meet my aunt at the airport.
   Ⓓ Let's meat for lunch next week.

4. Which sentence is written correctly?
   Ⓐ Look at that pretty pink flour.
   ● Chris added the flour while Jill stirred.
   Ⓒ I need three cups of flower for the cookies.
   Ⓓ Mark picked a white flour for his mother.

5. Which sentence is written correctly?
   Ⓐ I have curly hare.
   Ⓑ Tony has short hare.
   Ⓒ We saw a hair jump behind a tree.
   ● Sharon has long hair.

© Evan-Moor Corp. • EMC 2802 • Vocabulary Fundamentals 71

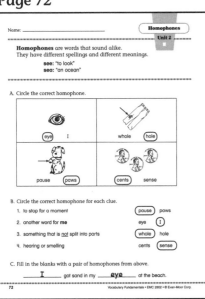

Name: _____

Homophones
Unit 2

Homophones are words that sound alike.
They have different spellings and different meanings.

see: "to look"
sea: "an ocean"

A. Circle the correct homophone.

| (eye) I | whole (hole) |
| pause (paws) | (cents) sense |

B. Circle the correct homophone for each clue.

1. to stop for a moment   (pause) paws
2. another word for **me**   eye (I)
3. something that is not split into parts   (whole) hole
4. hearing or smelling   cents (sense)

C. Fill in the blanks with a pair of homophones from above.

I got sand in my **eye** at the beach.

72 Vocabulary Fundamentals • EMC 2802 • © Evan-Moor Corp.

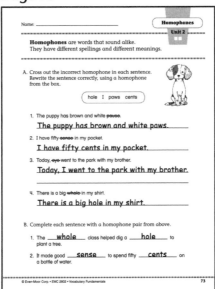

Name: _____

Homophones
Unit 2

Homophones are words that sound alike.
They have different spellings and different meanings.

A. Cross out the incorrect homophone in each sentence. Rewrite the sentence correctly, using a homophone from the box.

| hole | I | paws | cents |

1. The puppy has brown and white ~~pause~~.
   The puppy has brown and white paws.
2. I have fifty ~~sense~~ in my pocket.
   I have fifty cents in my pocket.
3. Today, ~~eye~~ went to the park with my brother.
   Today, I went to the park with my brother.
4. There is a big ~~whole~~ in my shirt.
   There is a big hole in my shirt.

B. Complete each sentence with a homophone pair from above.

1. The **whole** class helped dig a **hole** to plant a tree.
2. It made good **sense** to spend fifty **cents** on a bottle of water.

© Evan-Moor Corp. • EMC 2802 • Vocabulary Fundamentals 73

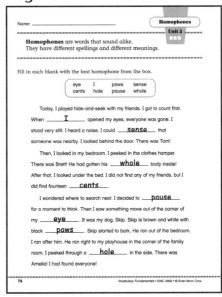

Name: _____

Homophones
Unit 3

Homophones are words that sound alike.
They have different spellings and different meanings.

Fill in each blank with the best homophone from the box.

| eye | I | paws | sense |
| cents | hole | pause | whole |

Today, I played hide-and-seek with my friends. I got to count first. When **I** opened my eyes, everyone was gone. I stood very still. I heard a noise. I could **sense** that someone was nearby. I looked behind the door. There was Tom!

Then, I looked in my bedroom. I peeked in the clothes hamper. There was Brett! He had gotten his **whole** body inside! After that, I looked under the bed. I did not find any of my friends, but I did find fourteen **cents**.

I wondered where to search next. I decided to **pause** for a moment to think. Then I saw something move out of the corner of my **eye**. It was my dog, Skip. Skip is brown and white with black **paws**. Skip started to bark. He ran out of the bedroom. I ran after him. He ran right to my playhouse in the corner of the family room. I peeked through a **hole** in the side. There was Amelia! I had found everyone!

74 Vocabulary Fundamentals • EMC 2802 • © Evan-Moor Corp.

Page 75

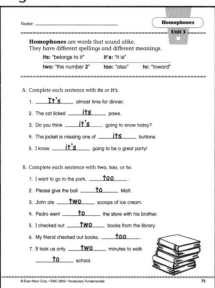

Name: _____

Homophones
Unit 3

Homophones are words that sound alike.
They have different spellings and different meanings.

its: "belongs to it" **it's:** "it is"
two: "the number 2" **too:** "also" **to:** "toward"

A. Complete each sentence with **its** or **it's**.
1. __It's__ almost time for dinner.
2. The cat licked __its__ paws.
3. Do you think __it's__ going to snow today?
4. The jacket is missing one of __its__ buttons.
5. I know __it's__ going to be a great party!

B. Complete each sentence with **two**, **too**, or **to**.
1. I want to go to the park, __too__.
2. Please give the ball __to__ Matt.
3. John ate __two__ scoops of ice cream.
4. Pedro went __to__ the store with his brother.
5. I checked out __two__ books from the library.
6. My friend checked out books, __too__.
7. It took us only __two__ minutes to walk __to__ school.

Page 76

Name: _____

Homophones
Unit 3

Homophones are words that sound alike.
They have different spellings and different meanings.

its: "belongs to it" **it's:** "it is"
two: "the number 2" **too:** "also" **to:** "toward"

A. Cross out the incorrect homophone in each sentence.
Write the correct homophone on the line.
1. I would like a cookie, ~~to~~. __too__
2. We have ~~too~~ kittens. __two__
3. Can we go ~~two~~ Grandma's house now? __to__
4. I know how to ride a bike, ~~two~~. __too__
5. Maria did all her chores, ~~to~~. __too__
6. I brought ~~too~~ pencils to school. __two__

B. Write a sentence using each homophone.
Underline the homophone.
1. Its: __Sentences will vary.__
2. It's: _____

Page 77

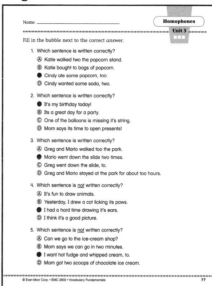

Name: _____

Homophones
Unit 3

Fill in the bubble next to the correct answer.
1. Which sentence is written correctly?
   Ⓐ Katie walked two the popcorn stand.
   Ⓑ Katie bought to bags of popcorn.
   ● Cindy ate some popcorn, too.
   Ⓓ Cindy wanted some soda, two.
2. Which sentence is written correctly?
   ● It's my birthday today!
   Ⓑ Its a great day for a party.
   Ⓒ One of the balloons is missing it's string.
   Ⓓ Mom says its time to open presents!
3. Which sentence is written correctly?
   Ⓐ Greg and Mario walked too the park.
   ● Mario went down the slide two times.
   Ⓒ Greg went down the slide, to.
   Ⓓ Greg and Mario stayed at the park for about too hours.
4. Which sentence is **not** written correctly?
   Ⓐ It's fun to draw animals.
   Ⓑ Yesterday, I drew a cat licking its paws.
   ● I had a hard time drawing it's ears.
   Ⓓ I think it's a good picture.
5. Which sentence is **not** written correctly?
   Ⓐ Can we go to the ice-cream shop?
   Ⓑ Mom says we can go in two minutes.
   ● I want hot fudge and whipped cream, to.
   Ⓓ Mom got two scoops of chocolate ice cream.

Page 78

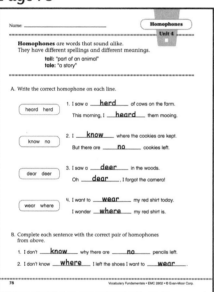

Name: _____

Homophones
Unit 4

Homophones are words that sound alike.
They have different spellings and different meanings.

tail: "part of an animal"
tale: "a story"

A. Write the correct homophone on each line.

[heard herd]
1. I saw a __herd__ of cows on the farm.
   This morning, I __heard__ them mooing.

[know no]
2. I __know__ where the cookies are kept.
   But there are __no__ cookies left.

[dear deer]
3. I saw a __deer__ in the woods.
   Oh __dear__, I forgot the camera!

[wear where]
4. I want to __wear__ my red shirt today.
   I wonder __where__ my red shirt is.

B. Complete each sentence with the correct pair of homophones from above.
1. I don't __know__ why there are __no__ pencils left.
2. I don't know __where__ I left the shoes I want to __wear__.

Page 79

Name: _____

Homophones
Unit 4

Homophones are words that sound alike.
They have different spellings and different meanings.

A. Write a sentence using each homophone.
Underline the homophone in each sentence.
1. no: __Sentences will vary but must contain the appropriate homophones.__
2. know: _____
3. herd: _____
4. heard: _____
5. dear: _____
6. deer: _____

B. Write a sentence using the homophones **where** and **wear**.
Underline the homophones in the sentence.
__Sentences will vary but must contain the appropriate homophones.__

Page 80

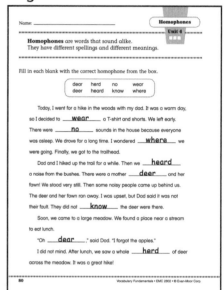

Name: _____

Homophones
Unit 4

Homophones are words that sound alike.
They have different spellings and different meanings.

Fill in each blank with the correct homophone from the box.

[dear herd no wear]
[deer heard know where]

Today, I went for a hike in the woods with my dad. It was a warm day, so I decided to __wear__ a T-shirt and shorts. We left early. There were __no__ sounds in the house because everyone was asleep. We drove for a long time. I wondered __where__ we were going. Finally, we got to the trailhead.

Dad and I hiked up the trail for a while. Then we __heard__ a noise from the bushes. There were a mother __deer__ and her fawn! We stood very still. Then some noisy people came up behind us. The deer and her fawn ran away. I was upset, but Dad said it was not their fault. They did not __know__ the deer were there.

Soon, we came to a large meadow. We found a place near a stream to eat lunch.

"Oh __dear__," said Dad. "I forgot the apples."

I did not mind. After lunch, we saw a whole __herd__ of deer across the meadow. It was a great hike!

Page 81

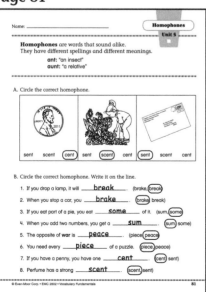

Name: _____

Homophones
Unit 5

Homophones are words that sound alike.
They have different spellings and different meanings.

ant: "an insect"
aunt: "a relative"

A. Circle the correct homophone.

sent scent (cent)   sent (scent) cent   (sent) scent cent

B. Circle the correct homophone. Write it on the line.
1. If you drop a lamp, it will __break__. (brake, break)
2. When you stop a car, you __brake__. (brake, break)
3. If you eat part of a pie, you eat __some__ of it. (sum, some)
4. When you add two numbers, you get a __sum__. (sum, some)
5. The opposite of war is __peace__. (piece, peace)
6. You need every __piece__ of a puzzle. (piece, peace)
7. If you have a penny, you have one __cent__. (cent, sent)
8. Perfume has a strong __scent__. (scent, sent)

Page 82

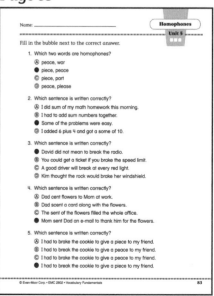

Name: _____

Homophones
Unit 5

Homophones are words that sound alike.
They have different spellings and different meanings.

A. Complete each sentence with the correct homophone from the box.

[piece sum sent scent]
[peace some cent]

1. I added the numbers to get the correct __sum__.
2. Tara had a __piece__ of chocolate cake.
3. My grandma __sent__ me a birthday gift.
4. Mom said she just wanted five minutes of __peace__.
5. The garden was filled with the __scent__ of roses.
6. I brought __some__ cookies to school to share.
7. You cannot buy much if you only have one __cent__.

B. Write a sentence using each homophone.
Underline the homophone.
1. break: __Sentences will vary but must contain the appropriate homophones.__
2. brake: _____

Page 83

Name: _____

Homophones
Unit 5

Fill in the bubble next to the correct answer.
1. Which two words are homophones?
   Ⓐ peace, war
   ● piece, peace
   Ⓒ piece, part
   Ⓓ peace, please
2. Which sentence is written correctly?
   Ⓐ I did sum of my math homework this morning.
   Ⓑ I had to add sum numbers together.
   ● Some of the problems were easy.
   Ⓓ I added 6 plus 4 and got a sum of 10.
3. Which sentence is written correctly?
   ● David did not mean to break the radio.
   Ⓑ You could get a ticket if you brake the speed limit.
   Ⓒ A good driver will break at every red light.
   Ⓓ Kim thought the rock would brake her windshield.
4. Which sentence is written correctly?
   Ⓐ Dad cent flowers to Mom at work.
   Ⓑ Dad scent a card along with the flowers.
   Ⓒ The sent of the flowers filled the whole office.
   ● Mom sent Dad an e-mail to thank him for the flowers.
5. Which sentence is written correctly?
   Ⓐ I had to brake the cookie to give a piece to my friend.
   Ⓑ I had to break the cookie to give a peace to my friend.
   Ⓒ I had to break the cookie to give a peace to my friend.
   ● I had to break the cookie to give a piece to my friend.

Page 84

Name: _____

Homophones
Unit 6

Homophones are words that sound alike.
They have different spellings and different meanings.
   right: "correct"
   write: "to make words with a pencil"

A. Write the correct homophone on each line.

1. Tony walked down the ___hall___ to his classroom.
   (hall, haul)

   Maria had to ___haul___ the heavy books home.
   (hall, haul)

2. Tom went outside to chop some ___wood___ for the fire.
   (wood, would)

   Lucy knew it ___would___ be a great day.
   (wood, would)

3. Nathan wore his ___red___ shirt to the party.
   (red, read)

   Danny ___read___ a book on the bus.
   (red, read)

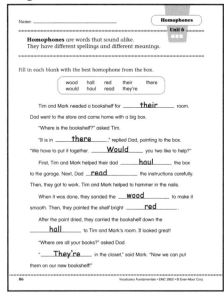

B. Write a sentence using the homophones **would** and **wood**.

Sentences will vary but must contain the
appropriate homophones.

84

Page 85

Name: _____

Homophones
Unit 6

Homophones are words that sound alike.
They have different spellings and different meanings.
   their: "belonging to them"
   they're: "they are"
   there: "a location or place"

A. Write **their**, **they're**, or **there** on each line.

1. I can see them over ___there___.
2. The children left ___their___ coats inside.
3. ___They're___ all going to the movies tonight.
4. Ben and Mary like sprinkles on ___their___ ice cream.
5. We will be able to see the parade if we stand over ___there___.
6. I think ___they're___ all ready now.

B. Cross out the incorrect homophones in each sentence.
Rewrite the sentence correctly.

1. ~~There~~ all waiting over ~~their~~.
   They're all waiting over there.

2. ~~Their~~ putting ~~there~~ shoes on over ~~they're~~.
   They're putting their shoes on over there.

© Evan-Moor Corp. • EMC 2802 • Vocabulary Fundamentals   85

Page 86

Name: _____

Homophones
Unit 6

Homophones are words that sound alike.
They have different spellings and different meanings.

Fill in each blank with the best homophone from the box.

| wood | hall | red | their |
| would | haul | read | they're |

Tim and Mark needed a bookshelf for ___their___ room.

Dad went to the store and came home with a big box.

   "Where is the bookshelf?" asked Tim.

   "It is in ___there___," replied Dad, pointing to the box.

"We have to put it together. ___Would___ you two like to help?"

First, Tim and Mark helped their dad ___haul___ the box

to the garage. Next, Dad ___read___ the instructions carefully.

Then, they got to work. Tim and Mark helped to hammer in the nails.

   When it was done, they sanded the ___wood___ to make it

smooth. Then, they painted the shelf bright ___red___.

   After the paint dried, they carried the bookshelf down the

___hall___ to Tim and Mark's room. It looked great!

   "Where are all your books?" asked Dad.

   "___They're___ in the closet," said Mark. "Now we can put

them on our new bookshelf!"

86

Page 87

Name: _____

Homographs
Unit 1

Homographs are words that are spelled the same
but have different meanings.
   A **duck** can be a kind of bird.
   You might **duck** to avoid being hit by something.

Read each pair of sentences.
Match each sentence to the correct picture.

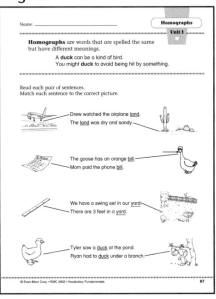

Drew watched the airplane **land**.
The **land** was dry and sandy.

The goose has an orange **bill**.
Mom paid the phone **bill**.

We have a swing set in our **yard**.
There are 3 feet in a **yard**.

Tyler saw a **duck** at the pond.
Ryan had to **duck** under a branch.

© Evan-Moor Corp. • EMC 2802 • Vocabulary Fundamentals   87

Page 88

Name: _____

Homographs
Unit 1

Homographs are words that are spelled the same
but have different meanings.

A. Read the two meanings for the underlined word.
Circle the meaning used in the sentence.

1. Jim's dad had to **duck** to get through the playhouse doorway.
   • (to bend down to avoid hitting something)
   • a kind of bird with webbed feet

2. The sailor saw **land** ahead.
   • to touch the ground
   • (part of the Earth not covered by water)

3. The waiter brought the **bill** to the table.
   • the beak of certain birds
   • (a piece of paper showing how much money a person owes)

4. Our yard has three trees and a lot of bushes.
   • (a grassy area near a house)
   • a unit of measure

B. Write your own sentences for each meaning of **duck**.

1. "to bend down quickly":
   Sentences will vary.

2. "a kind of bird":
   _____

88

Page 89

Name: _____

Homographs
Unit 1

Fill in the bubble next to the correct answer.

1. Which word has more than one meaning?
   Ⓐ owl
   ● duck
   Ⓒ rabbit
   Ⓓ lion

2. Which word does not have more than one meaning?
   Ⓐ yard
   Ⓑ bill
   ● car
   Ⓓ land

3. Which one is not a meaning of the word **land**?
   Ⓐ "a baby sheep"
   Ⓑ "to arrive by airplane"
   ● "part of the Earth not covered by water"
   Ⓓ "ground"

4. Which one is not a meaning of the word **bill**?
   Ⓐ "a piece of paper showing how much money someone owes"
   Ⓑ "the beak of a duck"
   ● "a green vegetable"
   Ⓓ "the beak of a goose"

5. Which sentence is not about a grassy area near a house?
   Ⓐ Tara and Anne have a sandbox in their yard.
   Ⓑ Our yard is not very big.
   Ⓒ We have a fence so that our dog cannot get out of the yard.
   ● I trained to run the 50-yard dash.

© Evan-Moor Corp. • EMC 2802 • Vocabulary Fundamentals   89

Page 90

Name: _____

Homographs
Unit 2

Homographs are words that are spelled the same
but have different meanings.
   You can wash your hands in a **sink**.
   A rock will **sink** to the bottom of a lake.

Read each pair of sentences.
Match each sentence to the correct picture.

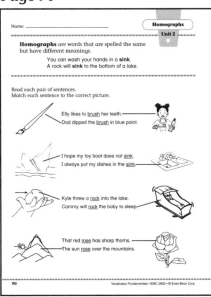

Elly likes to **brush** her teeth.
Dad dipped the **brush** in blue paint.

I hope my toy boat does not **sink**.
I always put my dishes in the **sink**.

Kyle threw a **rock** into the lake.
Cammy will **rock** the baby to sleep.

That red **rose** has sharp thorns.
The sun **rose** over the mountains.

90

Page 91

Name: _____

Homographs
Unit 2

Homographs are words that are spelled the same
but have different meanings.

A. Each sentence contains a pair of homographs.
Circle the homograph in the sentence that goes with the given meaning.

1. The sun (rose) over the rose garden.
   Meaning: "went to a higher place"

2. The spoons always (sink) when I wash dishes in the sink.
   Meaning: "to drop down underwater"

3. I brush my hair with a purple (brush).
   Meaning: "a tool with bristles and a handle"

B. Write your own sentences for each definition.

1. **sink**
   "a place to wash": Sentences will vary.

   "to drop down underwater": _____

2. **rock**
   "a stone": _____

   "to move back and forth": _____

© Evan-Moor Corp. • EMC 2802 • Vocabulary Fundamentals   91

Page 92

Name: _____

Homographs
Unit 2

Fill in the bubble next to the correct answer.

1. Which word has more than one meaning?
   ● brush
   Ⓑ toothpaste
   Ⓒ hair
   Ⓓ bath

2. Which word does not have more than one meaning?
   Ⓐ rock
   ● hat
   Ⓒ sink
   Ⓓ brush

3. Which one is not a meaning of the word **rock**?
   Ⓐ "a stone"
   Ⓑ "to move back and forth"
   Ⓒ "a way to move a baby"
   ● "hard"

4. Which one is not a meaning of the word **sink**?
   ● "a place to cook food"
   Ⓑ "to drop down underwater"
   Ⓒ "a place to wash your hands"
   Ⓓ "the opposite of **float**"

5. Which sentence is not about a flower?
   Ⓐ Mike watered the rosebush.
   Ⓑ Julie put the red rose in the blue vase.
   Ⓒ Kim thought the rose was beautiful.
   ● The moon rose high in the sky.

92

162   Vocabulary Fundamentals • EMC 2802 • © Evan-Moor Corp.

Page 93

Name: _____

Homographs — Unit 3

Homographs are words that are spelled the same but have different meanings.

If you did a good job on something, you did it **well**.
You can get water from a **well**.

A. Circle the sentence that goes with each picture.

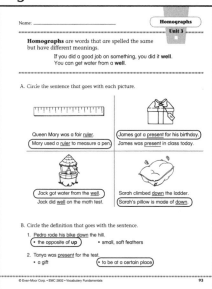

Queen Mary was a fair ruler.
Mary used a ruler to measure a pen.

James got a present for his birthday.
James was present in class today.

Jack got water from the well.
Jack did well on the math test.

Sarah climbed down the ladder.
Sarah's pillow is made of down.

B. Circle the definition that goes with the sentence.
1. Pedro rode his bike down the hill.
   the opposite of up • small, soft feathers
2. Tanya was present for the test.
   • a gift • **to be at a certain place**

© Evan-Moor Corp. • EMC 2802 • Vocabulary Fundamentals — 93

Page 94

Name: _____

Homographs — Unit 3

Homographs are words that are spelled the same but have different meanings.

A. Read each sentence.
Write the meaning of the underlined homograph.

1. Karen stayed home from school until she felt well.
   meaning: **not sick**

   Dan used a bucket to get water from the well.
   meaning: **a place/hole in the ground that holds water**

2. King Edward was loved by the people because he was a fair ruler.
   meaning: **a leader of a country**

   Jenny used a ruler to draw a straight line.
   meaning: **a measuring stick**

B. Write sentences using homographs.

1. Use **present**, meaning "gift."
   Sentences will vary.

2. Use **down**, the opposite of **up**.

94 — Vocabulary Fundamentals • EMC 2802 • © Evan-Moor Corp.

Page 95

Name: _____

Homographs — Unit 3

Fill in the bubble next to the correct answer.

1. Which word does not have more than one meaning?
   Ⓐ well
   Ⓑ down
   ● up
   Ⓓ ruler

2. Which one is not a meaning of the word well?
   Ⓐ "good"
   Ⓑ "a place to get diamonds"
   Ⓒ "a place to get water"
   Ⓓ "not sick"

3. Which one gives two meanings of the word down?
   Ⓐ "pillow," "slide"
   ● "not up," "feathers"
   Ⓒ "sink," "float"
   Ⓓ "jacket," "stairs"

4. Which sentence is about the leader of a country?
   Ⓐ I used a ruler to measure my foot.
   Ⓑ The principal buys the school rulers.
   ● King Harold was the ruler of Fabulasia for 50 years.
   Ⓓ My ruler is made of wood.

5. Which sentence is not about a gift?
   Ⓐ I picked out a special present for my friend Amber.
   Ⓑ I wrapped Amber's present in blue and red paper.
   ● I was present at Amber's birthday party.
   Ⓓ Amber said she liked the present I got her.

© Evan-Moor Corp. • EMC 2802 • Vocabulary Fundamentals — 95

Page 96

Name: _____

Homographs — Unit 4

Homographs are words that are spelled the same but have different meanings.

You can turn **left** at the corner.
You may have **left** your book at home.

Read each sentence.
Match the underlined homograph with its meaning in the box.
Write the letter on the line.

a. to be lazy
b. a baked shape

1. **b** Buy a loaf of wheat bread at the store.
2. **a** My family likes to loaf around on Saturday mornings.

a. a carnival
b. follows the rules

3. **a** We rode the Ferris wheel at the fair.
4. **b** I thought the game was not fair.

a. opposite of **heavy**
b. opposite of **dark**

5. **b** During summer, we stay outside as long as it's light.
6. **a** My backpack was easy to carry because it was so light.

96 — Vocabulary Fundamentals • EMC 2802 • © Evan-Moor Corp.

Page 97

Name: _____

Homographs — Unit 4

Homographs are words that are spelled the same but have different meanings.

Use each homograph in a sentence. Make sure that your sentence fits the definition.

1. **fair**
   "a carnival": **Sentences will vary.**

   "follows the rules": _____

2. **light**
   "not dark": _____

   "not heavy": _____

3. **left**
   "past tense of **leave**": _____

   "opposite of **right**": _____

© Evan-Moor Corp. • EMC 2802 • Vocabulary Fundamentals — 97

Page 98

Name: _____

Homographs — Unit 4

Fill in the bubble next to the correct answer.

1. Homographs are words that are spelled _____ .
   Ⓐ differently but have the same meaning
   Ⓑ differently and have different meanings
   ● the same but have different meanings
   Ⓓ the same and have the same meaning

2. Which one is not a meaning of the word fair?
   Ⓐ "a carnival"
   Ⓑ "a place with rides and animals"
   ● "to treat someone unkindly"
   Ⓓ "to play by following the rules"

3. Which one is not a meaning of the word light?
   ● "yellow"
   Ⓑ "not dark"
   Ⓒ "not heavy"
   Ⓓ "easy to lift"

4. Which sentence is about being lazy?
   Ⓐ Mom cut a slice from the loaf of bread.
   Ⓑ When the dough rises, the loaf is ready to bake.
   Ⓒ Nicky went to the store for a loaf of bread.
   ● My dad and brother like to loaf in front of the TV.

5. Which sentence is not about leaving something?
   Ⓐ I left my pencil on the desk.
   ● I write with my left hand.
   Ⓒ Todd left his little brother behind.
   Ⓓ I left two cookies for my sister.

98 — Vocabulary Fundamentals • EMC 2802 • © Evan-Moor Corp.

Page 99

Name: _____

Prefixes — Unit 1

A **prefix** is a word part added to the beginning of a base word. Adding a prefix changes the word's meaning.

The prefix **un–** means "not" or "the opposite of."

un– + welcome = **unwelcome** ("not wanted")
un– + pack = **unpack** ("the opposite of **pack**")

Add the prefix **un–** to make each new word.
Then circle the sentence that describes it.

1. **un** pack
   a. I put my clothes in the suitcase.
   b. I took my clothes out of the suitcase.

2. **un** kind
   a. That girl pushed me down.
   b. That girl helped me when I fell down.

3. **un** sure
   a. I know the answer to the question.
   b. I do not know the answer to the question.

4. **un** afraid
   a. That big dog is friendly and playful.
   b. That big dog might bite me!

5. **un** hurt
   a. I fell down and skinned my knee.
   b. I fell down, but I am okay.

6. **un** clear
   a. That game is hard to understand.
   b. That game is easy to play.

© Evan-Moor Corp. • EMC 2802 • Vocabulary Fundamentals — 99

Page 100

Name: _____

Prefixes — Unit 1

A **prefix** is a word part added to the beginning of a base word. Adding a prefix changes the word's meaning.

The prefix **un–** means "not" or "the opposite of."

Add the prefix **un–** to each bold word.
Then write a sentence using the new word.

1. wanted: **unwanted** = "not wanted"
   Sentences will vary.

2. important: **unimportant** = "not important"

3. healthy: **unhealthy** = "not healthy"

4. welcome: **unwelcome** = "not welcome"

100 — Vocabulary Fundamentals • EMC 2802 • © Evan-Moor Corp.

Page 101

Name: _____

Prefixes — Unit 1

A **prefix** is a word part added to the beginning of a base word. Adding a prefix changes the word's meaning.

Add un– to each word in the box. Think about the meanings.
Then choose the best word for each blank in the story.

| **un** hurt | **un** kind | **un** sure | **un** afraid |
| **un** healthy | **un** welcome | **un** pack | |

My family went on a picnic today! At first we were **unsure**
we would go because it looked like rain. But then the sky cleared up, and
the sun came out.

At the park, my sister and I raced to the picnic table. I slipped and fell,
but I was **unhurt** . Then I helped **unpack**
the picnic basket. We had sandwiches, watermelon, carrot sticks, and
brownies. Some people say brownies are **unhealthy** , but
Dad makes them with whole-wheat flour and honey.

We had some **unwelcome** guests while we were eating.
Lots of ants came! My sister was scared that they might bite her. I was
unafraid . I knew that they were not the kind that bite. She
wanted to smash the ants. Dad said that would be **unkind** .
The park is their home, not ours.

© Evan-Moor Corp. • EMC 2802 • Vocabulary Fundamentals — 101

Page 102

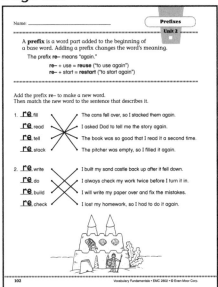

Name: _____

Prefixes
Unit 2

A **prefix** is a word part added to the beginning of a base word. Adding a prefix changes the word's meaning.

The prefix **re–** means "again."

re– + use = **reuse** ("to use again")
re– + start = **restart** ("to start again")

Add the prefix re– to make a new word.
Then match the new word to the sentence that describes it.

1. **re** fill — The cans fell over, so I stacked them again.
   re read — I asked Dad to tell me the story again.
   re tell — The book was so good that I read it a second time.
   re stack — The pitcher was empty, so I filled it again.

2. **re** write — I built my sand castle back up after it fell down.
   re do — I always check my work twice before I turn it in.
   re build — I will write my paper over and fix the mistakes.
   re check — I lost my homework, so I had to do it again.

Page 103

Prefixes
Unit 2

A **prefix** is a word part added to the beginning of a base word. Adding a prefix changes the word's meaning.

The prefix **re–** means "again."

A. Write the meaning of each word.

1. recheck: _to check again_
2. restack: _to stack again_
3. reuse: _to use again_
4. restart: _to start again_

B. Finish each sentence.

1. I had to <u>rewrite</u> my paper because _Sentences will vary._
2. We will <u>review</u> the new spelling words because _____
3. Kim had to <u>refill</u> the ice tray because _____
4. We had to <u>rebuild</u> the snow fort because _____
5. My sister asked me to <u>reread</u> the story because _____

Page 104

Prefixes
Unit 2

Fill in the bubble next to the correct answer.

1. The prefix re– means _____.
   Ⓐ "at"
   ● "again"
   Ⓒ "always"
   Ⓓ "above"

2. Which word means "to check again"?
   Ⓐ checker
   Ⓑ checkout
   Ⓒ uncheck
   ● recheck

3. If you did your homework incorrectly, what would you need to do?
   ● redo it
   Ⓑ refill it
   Ⓒ reuse it
   Ⓓ rearrange it

4. Which word does <u>not</u> contain the prefix re–?
   Ⓐ restack
   Ⓑ rewrite
   ● restful
   Ⓓ review

5. Which sentence is written correctly?
   ● I had to reread the test question.
   Ⓑ I had to read the retest question.
   Ⓒ I had to read the test requestion.
   Ⓓ I rehad to read the test question.

Page 105

Prefixes
Unit 3

A **prefix** is a word part added to the beginning of a base word. Adding a prefix changes the word's meaning.

The prefix **dis–** means "not" or "the opposite of."

dis– + connected = **disconnected** ("not connected")
dis– + believe = **disbelieve** ("the opposite of **believe**")

Add the prefix dis– to make a new word.
Then circle the sentence that describes it.

1. **dis** agree
   a. We both feel the same way about it.
   b. (Each of us feels differently about it.)

2. **dis** like
   a. (I do not enjoy doing math problems.)
   b. I enjoy doing math problems.

3. **dis** continue
   a. (I stopped reading the book.)
   b. I kept reading the book.

4. **dis** obey
   a. I followed the teacher's directions.
   b. (I did not follow the teacher's directions.)

5. **dis** interest
   a. (I do not want to learn more.)
   b. I want to learn more.

6. **dis** trust
   a. I know she is telling the truth.
   b. (I think she might be lying.)

Page 106

Prefixes
Unit 3

A **prefix** is a word part added to the beginning of a base word. Adding a prefix changes the word's meaning.

The prefix **dis–** means "not" or "the opposite of."

Add the prefix **dis–** to the <u>underlined</u> word in each sentence.
Then rewrite the sentence with the new word.

1. Mike's desk was in <u>order</u>. **dis** order
   Sentences will vary.
2. Lily wants to <u>connect</u> the wires. **dis** connect
3. Mom <u>approves</u> of eating in the living room. **dis** approves
4. I really <u>like</u> spinach and cabbage. **dis** like
5. The magician made the rabbit <u>appear</u>. **dis** appear

Page 107

Prefixes
Unit 3

A **prefix** is a word part added to the beginning of a base word. Adding a prefix changes the word's meaning.

Add dis– to each word in the box. Think about the meanings.
Then choose the best word for each blank in the story.

dis agree   **dis** obeys   **dis** like
dis appears   **dis** approves   **dis** continue

My new puppy, Junior, is a big problem! I know he's smart, but he never does what I say. If I call him to come in from the yard, he **disobeys** and **disappears** into the bushes. He barks all the time and has even dug up our flower bed. I know our neighbor, Mrs. Jones, **disapproves** of his behavior.

"Junior is a bad dog!" I told my dad.

"I **disagree**," said Dad. "If we want Junior to **discontinue** doing things we **dislike**, we have to teach him what to do."

Dad got a book on dog training, and we worked with Junior every day. He was a quick learner. Soon, he was the best-behaved dog on our block!

Page 108

Prefixes
Unit 4

A **prefix** is a word part added to the beginning of a base word. Adding a prefix changes the word's meaning.

The prefix **pre–** means "before."

pre– + pay = **prepay** ("to pay before")
pre– + heat = **preheat** ("to heat before")

A. Underline the prefix in each sentence.
Then write the base word on the line.

1. Be sure to <u>pre</u>heat the oven. pre + **heat**
2. We had to <u>pre</u>pay to buy our tickets. pre + **pay**
3. My little sister goes to <u>pre</u>school. pre + **school**
4. We watched the <u>pre</u>flight safety movie. pre + **flight**
5. The paper was <u>pre</u>cut for our art project. pre + **cut**

B. Add the prefix pre– to make a new word.
Then match the new word to the sentence that describes it.

1. **pre** board — The flour and the salt were already combined.
2. **pre** view — People with small children get on the plane first.
3. **pre** mix — I put on safety goggles before the experiment.
4. **pre** caution — We saw the movie before anyone else.

Page 109

Prefixes
Unit 4

A **prefix** is a word part added to the beginning of a base word. Adding a prefix changes the word's meaning.

The prefix **pre–** means "before."

A. Complete each sentence with a word from the box.

| prepay | prerecorded | preview | preheat |
| prebaked | prepackaged | preschool | precaution |

1. Timmy got to finger-paint in _preschool_ today.
2. The recipe said to _preheat_ the oven.
3. We watched the _prerecorded_ baseball game on TV.
4. The rolls were _prebaked_, so we only had to warm them.
5. It costs less to get into the fair if you _prepay_.
6. The _prepackaged_ cookies are either in boxes or paper bags.
7. We watched a movie _preview_ before the main show.
8. Amber took the _precaution_ of wearing a life vest.

B. Use a word from the box to write a sentence of your own.
Sentences will vary.

Page 110

Prefixes
Unit 4

Fill in the bubble next to the correct answer.

1. Which word has a prefix that means "before"?
   ● precut
   Ⓑ uncut
   Ⓒ undercut
   Ⓓ cutting

2. Which word means "to pay ahead of time"?
   Ⓐ paid
   Ⓑ overpay
   ● prepay
   Ⓓ payment

3. Which word means "to let the oven get hot before you bake something"?
   Ⓐ premix
   Ⓑ preview
   Ⓒ prebake
   ● preheat

4. Which word does <u>not</u> contain the prefix pre–?
   Ⓐ precaution
   ● president
   Ⓒ prerecorded
   Ⓓ prepackaged

5. Which sentence tells about a man boarding a plane before anyone else?
   ● The man was permitted to preboard the plane.
   Ⓑ The man was permitted to reboard the plane.
   Ⓒ The man was permitted to unboard the plane.
   Ⓓ The man was permitted to disboard the plane.

164

Page 111

Name: _____

Prefixes
Unit 5

A **prefix** is a word part added to the beginning of a base word. Adding a prefix changes the word's meaning.

The prefix **mis–** means "bad" or "wrong."

mis– + behavior = **misbehavior** ("bad behavior")
mis– + count = **miscount** ("to count incorrectly")

A. Add the prefix **mis–** to each underlined word. Write the new word on the line.

1. to lead someone in the wrong direction — **mislead**
2. to count something incorrectly — **miscount**
3. to judge someone wrongly — **misjudge**
4. to be badly informed — **misinformed**
5. to pronounce a word incorrectly — **mispronounce**
6. to put something in the wrong place — **misplace**

B. Circle the word in each sentence that has a prefix. Then write the base word on the line.

1. I try not to (misspell) words. — mis + **spell**
2. We will be late if I (misplace) the keys. — mis + **place**
3. I never (misbehave) in school. — mis + **behave**
4. Add carefully so you do not (miscalculate) the answer. — mis + **calculate**

© Evan-Moor Corp. • EMC 2802 • Vocabulary Fundamentals 111

Page 112

Name: _____

Prefixes
Unit 5

A **prefix** is a word part added to the beginning of a base word. Adding a prefix changes the word's meaning.

The prefix **mis–** means "bad" or "wrong."

A. Write the word from the box to match each definition.

| misplace | misspell | mislabel |
| misbehave | mismatch | mistreat |

1. to put on the wrong label — **mislabel**
2. to spell *cat* this way: k-a-t — **misspell**
3. to throw popcorn at a movie — **misbehave**
4. to pair a red sock with a blue one — **mismatch**
5. to forget where you put something — **misplace**
6. to be mean to someone or something — **mistreat**

B. Use each word in a sentence.

1. misbehave: _**Sentences will vary.**_

2. miscalculate: _____

3. misunderstand: _____

112 Vocabulary Fundamentals • EMC 2802 • © Evan-Moor Corp.

Page 113

Name: _____

Prefixes
Unit 5

A **prefix** is a word part added to the beginning of a base word. Adding a prefix changes the word's meaning.

Add the prefix **mis–** to each word in the box. Think about the meanings. Then choose the best word for each blank in the story.

| **mis** placed | **mis** judged | **mis** treated | **mis** match |
| **mis** calculated | **mis** pronounce | **mis** understand | **mis** behaving |

My family is from Mexico. When we first came to the United States, I did not know very much English. Whenever I talked to someone, I would often **mispronounce** a lot of words. Sometimes, other kids would **misunderstand** me. It was hard to make friends.

A boy named Kyle **mistreated** me because I was different. One day, the teacher caught him **misbehaving**. She said that we had to learn to get along. She made us work together in math. What a **mismatch**! At first, Kyle got angry at me because I **misplaced** my pencil and tried to borrow his. Then things got better. I saw that Kyle made a lot of mistakes on a test. He had **miscalculated** some of the subtraction problems. I showed him an easy way to do them. That made him happy. Soon, Kyle and I became friends! He said he was sorry for being mean to me and that he had **misjudged** me.

© Evan-Moor Corp. • EMC 2802 • Vocabulary Fundamentals 113

Page 114

Name: _____

Prefixes
Unit 6

A **prefix** is a word part added to the beginning of a base word. Adding a prefix changes the word's meaning.

The prefix **over–** means "too much."

over– + pay = **overpay** ("to pay too much")
over– + weight = **overweight** ("to weigh too much")

A. Add the prefix **over–** to make a new word. Then match the new word to its meaning.

1. **over** cook — to pay too much
2. **over** do — to spend too much
3. **over** pay — to cook too much
4. **over** spend — to do too much

B. Circle each word with a prefix. Then write the prefix and the base word on the lines.

1. Dad was tired and (overworked). — **over** + **worked**
2. That library book is (overdue). — **over** + **due**
3. Try not to (overload) the wheelbarrow. — **over** + **load**
4. The room was (overcrowded). — **over** + **crowded**
5. If you (overwater) the plant, it might die. — **over** + **water**
6. It is hard not to (overeat) at a party. — **over** + **eat**

114 Vocabulary Fundamentals • EMC 2802 • © Evan-Moor Corp.

Page 115

Name: _____

Prefixes
Unit 6

A **prefix** is a word part added to the beginning of a base word. Adding a prefix changes the word's meaning.

The prefix **over–** means "too much."

A. Complete each sentence with a word from the box.

| overload | overdue | overdo | overactive |
| overcrowded | overcook | overspend | overwater |

1. Dad did not want to **overspend** in order to buy a new car.
2. It's hard to get my **overactive** little brother to sit still for a meal.
3. I must go to the library today because my book is **overdue**.
4. On your first hike, don't **overdo** it by walking too far.
5. It is easy to **overwater** a cactus plant.
6. If you **overload** your backpack, it will be hard to carry.
7. The desks were wall-to-wall in the **overcrowded** classroom.
8. If you **overcook** the meat, it will get tough.

B. Use a word from the box to write a sentence of your own.

_____ **Sentences will vary.** _____

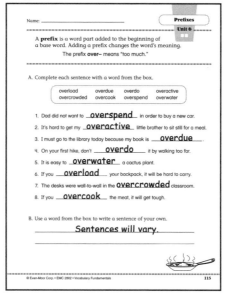

© Evan-Moor Corp. • EMC 2802 • Vocabulary Fundamentals 115

Page 116

Name: _____

Prefixes
Unit 6

Fill in the bubble next to the correct answer.

1. A prefix is a word part _____.
   Ⓐ added to the end of a base word to make a new word
   ● added to the beginning of a base word to make a new word
   Ⓒ added to the middle of a base word to make a new word
   Ⓓ that sounds like another word

2. Which of these means "to cook something too much"?
   Ⓐ precook
   Ⓑ recook
   ● overcook
   Ⓓ miscook

3. If a bus is so full that people are standing up, the bus is _____.
   Ⓐ discrowded
   Ⓑ uncrowded
   Ⓒ miscrowded
   ● overcrowded

4. If your father gives you $500 to mow the lawn, you have been _____.
   ● overpaid
   Ⓑ unpaid
   Ⓒ mispaid
   Ⓓ repaid

5. Which sentence is written correctly?
   Ⓐ If you reload a box, it could be too heavy to lift.
   Ⓑ If you preload a box, it could be too heavy to lift.
   ● If you overload a box, it could be too heavy to lift.
   Ⓓ If you unload a box, it could be too heavy to lift.

116 Vocabulary Fundamentals • EMC 2802 • © Evan-Moor Corp.

Page 117

Name: _____

Prefixes
Unit 7

A **prefix** is a word part added to the beginning of a base word. Adding a prefix changes the word's meaning.

The prefix **under–** means "beneath" or "not enough."

under– + water = **underwater** ("beneath the water")
under– + charge = **undercharge** ("to not charge enough")

A. Add the prefix **under–** to each base word. Then match the new word to its meaning.

1. **under** ground — not cooked enough
2. **under** fed — underwear
3. **under** paid — below the ground
4. **under** line — not given enough food
5. **under** cooked — not paid enough
6. **under** shirt — to draw a line beneath

B. Fill in each blank with a word from above.

1. I did not want to eat the **undercooked** hamburger.
2. The teacher said to **underline** our spelling words in the sentences.
3. Dad wears an **undershirt** every day.
4. We could tell the kitten was **underfed**, because it was so thin.
5. **Underground** pipes bring water to your home.
6. Tony asked for more money because he was being **underpaid**.

© Evan-Moor Corp. • EMC 2802 • Vocabulary Fundamentals 117

Page 118

Name: _____

Prefixes
Unit 7

A **prefix** is a word part added to the beginning of a base word. Adding a prefix changes the word's meaning.

The prefix **under–** means "beneath" or "not enough."

A. Fill in each blank with a word from the box.

| underfoot | underline | underwater | underpriced | undercover |

1. If you draw a line beneath a word, you **underline** it.
2. If something is being sold for less than it is worth, it is **underpriced**.
3. If you keep tripping on something, it is **underfoot**.
4. A deep-sea diver swims **underwater**.
5. The detective went **undercover** to catch a thief.

B. Use each word in a sentence.

1. underwater: _**Sentences will vary.**_

2. underpriced: _____

3. underfoot: _____

118 Vocabulary Fundamentals • EMC 2802 • © Evan-Moor Corp.

Page 119

Name: _____

Prefixes
Unit 7

A **prefix** is a word part added to the beginning of a base word. Adding a prefix changes the word's meaning.

Add the prefix **under–** to each word in the box. Think about the meanings. Then choose the best word for each blank in the story.

| **under** lined | **under** foot | **under** cooked |
| **under** ground | **under** priced | **under** cover |

Today, my mom took me with her to the grocery store. First, my mom got a pound of ground beef. The butcher reminded her to cook it for at least ten minutes so it would not be **undercooked**.

Then, Mom got out her pen and **underlined** three things on the shopping list. She gave the list to me and sent me off to find them. I pretended to be an **undercover** secret agent looking for clues. The first thing I found was the carrots. (I think it is neat how carrots grow **underground**.) Then, I went to look for bread. I picked an **underpriced** loaf that was on sale. I got the milk next and then met my mom at the checkout.

On the way to our car, I tripped on a rock that was **underfoot** and scraped my knee. Luckily, we had bought bandages at the store!

© Evan-Moor Corp. • EMC 2802 • Vocabulary Fundamentals 119

© Evan-Moor Corp. • EMC 2802 • Vocabulary Fundamentals

Page 120

Suffixes
Unit 1

A **suffix** is a word part added to the end of a base word.
Adding a suffix makes a new word.

The suffixes **–er** and **–or** mean "a person who."

teach + **–er** = **teacher** ("a person who teaches")
sail + **–or** = **sailor** ("a person who sails")

A. Read each word. Circle the suffix.
Match the word to the correct picture.

1. bak**er**
2. sail**or**
3. play**er**
4. farm**er**

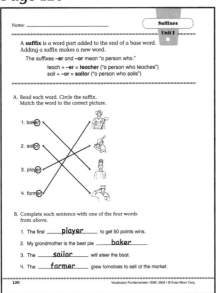

B. Complete each sentence with one of the four words from above.

1. The first **player** to get 50 points wins.
2. My grandmother is the best pie **baker**.
3. The **sailor** will steer the boat.
4. The **farmer** grew tomatoes to sell at the market.

120   Vocabulary Fundamentals • EMC 2802 • © Evan-Moor Corp.

Page 121

Name: _____

Suffixes
Unit 1

A **suffix** is a word part added to the end of a base word.
Adding a suffix makes a new word.

The suffixes **–er** and **–or** mean "a person who."

Choose the correct –er or –or word from the box to answer each riddle.

| painter | actor | pitcher | server | doctor |
| builder | worker | author | inventor | operator |

1. You see me when you watch movies. Who am I? **actor**
2. I bring you food at a restaurant. Who am I? **server**
3. I think up new things. Who am I? **inventor**
4. I can make your house a new color. Who am I? **painter**
5. I can be any person who does a job. Who am I? **worker**
6. You can thank me for your favorite book. Who am I? **author**
7. I can make new houses. Who am I? **builder**
8. I'll throw the ball to you. Who am I? **pitcher**
9. I help you to make phone calls. Who am I? **operator**
10. You visit me if you are sick. Who am I? **doctor**

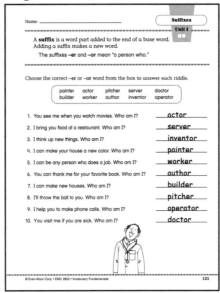

© Evan-Moor Corp. • EMC 2802 • Vocabulary Fundamentals   121

Page 122

Name: _____

Suffixes
Unit 1

Fill in the bubble next to the correct answer.

1. A suffix is a word part _____.
   - Ⓐ added to the beginning of a base word
   - ● added to the end of a base word
   - Ⓒ that is a word by itself
   - Ⓓ that makes a compound word

2. Which two suffixes mean "a person who"?
   - Ⓐ –er, –ed
   - Ⓑ –or, –ar
   - ● –er, –or
   - Ⓓ –or, –ur

3. The word **farmer** means _____.
   - Ⓐ "a place where vegetables are grown"
   - ● "a person who works on a farm"
   - Ⓒ "about the same as **barn**"
   - Ⓓ "a person who sells things"

4. Which word does not name a person who does something?
   - Ⓐ author
   - Ⓑ doctor
   - Ⓒ actor
   - ● elevator

5. Which word best completes this sentence?
   The 911 _____ sent the fire engines to the burning building.
   - Ⓐ inventor
   - Ⓑ server
   - ● operator
   - Ⓓ teacher

122   Vocabulary Fundamentals • EMC 2802 • © Evan-Moor Corp.

Page 123

Name: _____

Suffixes
Unit 2

A **suffix** is a word part added to the end of a base word.
Adding a suffix makes a new word.
The suffix **–ful** means "full of."

color + **–ful** = **colorful** ("full of color")
pain + **–ful** = **painful** ("full of pain")

A. Use the suffix **–ful** to make a word for each definition.

1. full of care **careful**
2. full of cheer **cheerful**
3. full of help **helpful**
4. full of power **powerful**
5. full of delight **delightful**
6. full of color **colorful**
7. full of skill **skillful**
8. full of pain **painful**

B. Complete each sentence with a word from above.

1. Tim used the **powerful** backhoe to move the rocks.
2. Doing the dishes is one way to be **helpful** at home.
3. Katie used a lot of crayons to draw a **colorful** picture.
4. The sunny day put everyone in a **cheerful** mood.
5. Andy took a **painful** fall off his bike.
6. Everyone had a **delightful** time at the party.
7. Scott is a **skillful** soccer player because he practices.
8. Adults should be **careful** when lighting a fire.

© Evan-Moor Corp. • EMC 2802 • Vocabulary Fundamentals   123

Page 124

Name: _____

Suffixes
Unit 2

A **suffix** is a word part added to the end of a base word.
Adding a suffix makes a new word.
The suffix **–ful** means "full of."

Add the suffix **–ful** to each base word.
Then write a sentence with the new word.

1. thank**ful**
   Sentences will vary.

2. help**ful**

3. play**ful**

4. use**ful**

5. forget**ful**

124   Vocabulary Fundamentals • EMC 2802 • © Evan-Moor Corp.

Page 125

Name: _____

Suffixes
Unit 2

A **suffix** is a word part added to the end of a base word.
Adding a suffix makes a new word.

Add –ful to each word in the box. Think about the meanings.
Then choose the best word for each blank in the story.

| play**ful** | thank**ful** | care**ful** | skill**ful** |
| color**ful** | cheer**ful** | thought**ful** | use**ful** |

My aunt gave me a big box of colored pencils for my birthday. She knows I want to be an artist when I grow up, so it was a **thoughtful** gift. I told her how **thankful** I was to have so many colored pencils. She told me that if I work hard, I will be a **skillful** artist someday.

I decided to draw a **colorful** picture for my aunt. I drew a kitten playing with a ball of yarn. I tried to be **careful** with my new pencils, but I broke one of the tips. Luckily, there was a sharpener in the box. I break pencil tips a lot, so I know that sharpener will be very **useful**.

My aunt loved the picture! She said she would put it in her kitchen because seeing that **playful** kitten would put her in a **cheerful** mood every morning.

© Evan-Moor Corp. • EMC 2802 • Vocabulary Fundamentals   125

Page 126

Name: _____

Suffixes
Unit 3

A **suffix** is a word part added to the end of a base word.
Adding a suffix makes a new word.
The suffix **–less** means "without."

fear + **–less** = **fearless** ("without fear")
worth + **–less** = **worthless** ("without worth")

Add the suffix **–less** to make a new word.
Then circle the sentence that describes it.

1. pain**less**
   a. It hurt a lot.
   ● b. It did not hurt at all.

2. sleep**less**
   ● a. I could not fall asleep.
   b. I slept all night long.

3. thought**less**
   ● a. She never thinks about other people.
   b. She always thinks about other people.

4. use**less**
   a. We used it every day.
   ● b. It was broken, so we never used it.

5. harm**less**
   ● a. That dog would never bite anyone.
   b. That dog bit someone yesterday.

6. tire**less**
   a. The men stopped to rest.
   ● b. The men marched all night long.

126   Vocabulary Fundamentals • EMC 2802 • © Evan-Moor Corp.

Page 127

Name: _____

Suffixes
Unit 3

A **suffix** is a word part added to the end of a base word.
Adding a suffix makes a new word.
The suffix **–less** means "without."

Replace the underlined phrase with a word that ends with the suffix –less.
Rewrite each sentence.

1. The computer was so old that it was without worth.
   The computer was so old that it was worthless.

2. The boring movie seemed to be without end.
   The boring movie seemed to be endless.

3. I was afraid, but my brother was without fear.
   I was afraid, but my brother was fearless.

4. The diamond was so big that it was without a price.
   The diamond was so big that it was priceless.

5. I was without care when I broke my friend's robot.
   I was careless when I broke my friend's robot.

© Evan-Moor Corp. • EMC 2802 • Vocabulary Fundamentals   127

Page 128

Name: _____

Suffixes
Unit 3

Fill in the bubble next to the correct answer.

1. The suffix **–less** means _____.
   - Ⓐ "full of"
   - Ⓑ "less than"
   - Ⓒ "already"
   - ● "without"

2. Which word means "without hope"?
   - Ⓐ hopeful
   - Ⓑ hoped
   - ● hopeless
   - Ⓓ hoping

3. Which word does not contain the suffix –less?
   - Ⓐ endless
   - ● bless
   - Ⓒ sleepless
   - Ⓓ priceless

4. Which sentence is written correctly?
   - Ⓐ The broken hammer was using.
   - ● The broken hammer was useless.
   - Ⓒ The broken hammer was user.
   - Ⓓ The broken hammer was useness.

5. Which of these is the correct way to divide the word **thoughtless** into a base word and a suffix?
   - Ⓐ though | tless
   - Ⓑ thought | ess
   - ● thought | less
   - Ⓓ thou | ghtless

128   Vocabulary Fundamentals • EMC 2802 • © Evan-Moor Corp.

Page 129

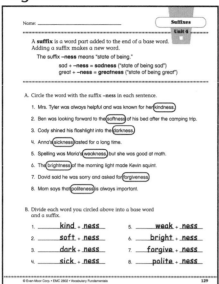

Name: _____

Suffixes — **Unit 4**

A **suffix** is a word part added to the end of a base word. Adding a suffix makes a new word.

The suffix **–ness** means "state of being."

sad + **–ness** = **sadness** ("state of being sad")
great + **–ness** = **greatness** ("state of being great")

A. Circle the word with the suffix –ness in each sentence.

1. Mrs. Tyler was always helpful and was known for her (kindness).
2. Ben was looking forward to the (softness) of his bed after the camping trip.
3. Cody shined his flashlight into the (darkness).
4. Anna's (sickness) lasted for a long time.
5. Spelling was Maria's (weakness) but she was good at math.
6. The (brightness) of the morning light made Kevin squint.
7. David said he was sorry and asked for (forgiveness).
8. Mom says that (politeness) is always important.

B. Divide each word you circled above into a base word and a suffix.

1. kind + ness
2. soft + ness
3. dark + ness
4. sick + ness
5. weak + ness
6. bright + ness
7. forgive + ness
8. polite + ness

© Evan-Moor Corp. • EMC 2802 • Vocabulary Fundamentals — 129

Page 130

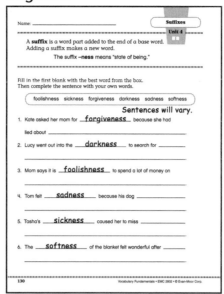

Name: _____

Suffixes — **Unit 4**

A **suffix** is a word part added to the end of a base word. Adding a suffix makes a new word.

The suffix **–ness** means "state of being."

Fill in the first blank with the best word from the box.
Then complete the sentence with your own words.

foolishness   sickness   forgiveness   darkness   sadness   softness

Sentences will vary.

1. Kate asked her mom for **forgiveness** because she had lied about _____

2. Lucy went out into the **darkness** to search for _____

3. Mom says it is **foolishness** to spend a lot of money on _____

4. Tom felt **sadness** because his dog _____

5. Tasha's **sickness** caused her to miss _____

6. The **softness** of the blanket felt wonderful after _____

130 — Vocabulary Fundamentals • EMC 2802 • © Evan-Moor Corp.

Page 131

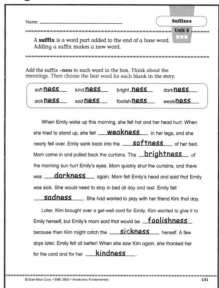

Name: _____

Suffixes — **Unit 4**

A **suffix** is a word part added to the end of a base word. Adding a suffix makes a new word.

Add the suffix –ness to each word in the box. Think about the meanings. Then choose the best word for each blank in the story.

soft**ness**   kind**ness**   bright**ness**   dark**ness**
sick**ness**   sad**ness**   foolish**ness**   weak**ness**

When Emily woke up this morning, she felt hot and her head hurt. When she tried to stand up, she felt **weakness** in her legs, and she nearly fell over. Emily sank back into the **softness** of her bed. Mom came in and pulled back the curtains. The **brightness** of the morning sun hurt Emily's eyes. Mom quickly shut the curtains, and there was **darkness** again. Mom felt Emily's head and said that Emily was sick. She would need to stay in bed all day and rest. Emily felt **sadness**. She had wanted to play with her friend Kim that day.

Later, Kim brought over a get-well card for Emily. Kim wanted to give it to Emily herself, but Emily's mom said that would be **foolishness** because then Kim might catch the **sickness** herself. A few days later, Emily felt all better! When she saw Kim again, she thanked her for the card and for her **kindness**.

© Evan-Moor Corp. • EMC 2802 • Vocabulary Fundamentals — 131

Page 133

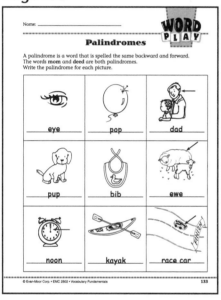

Name: _____

Palindromes

A palindrome is a word that is spelled the same backward and forward. The words **mom** and **deed** are both palindromes. Write the palindrome for each picture.

eye	pop	dad
pup	bib	ewe
noon	kayak	race car

© Evan-Moor Corp. • EMC 2802 • Vocabulary Fundamentals — 133

Page 134

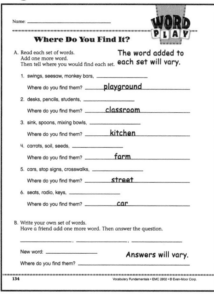

Name: _____

Where Do You Find It?

A. Read each set of words. Add one more word. Then tell where you would find each set.

The word added to each set will vary.

1. swings, seesaw, monkey bars, _____
   Where do you find them? **playground**

2. desks, pencils, students, _____
   Where do you find them? **classroom**

3. sink, spoons, mixing bowls, _____
   Where do you find them? **kitchen**

4. carrots, soil, seeds, _____
   Where do you find them? **farm**

5. cars, stop signs, crosswalks, _____
   Where do you find them? **street**

6. seats, radio, keys, _____
   Where do you find them? **car**

B. Write your own set of words. Have a friend add one more word. Then answer the question.

New word: ___ , ___ , ___

Answers will vary.

Where do you find them? _____

134 — Vocabulary Fundamentals • EMC 2802 • © Evan-Moor Corp.

Page 135

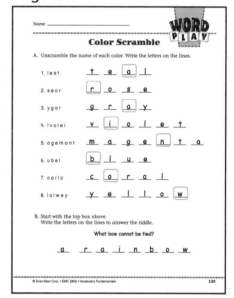

Name: _____

Color Scramble

A. Unscramble the name of each color. Write the letters on the lines.

1. leat — t e a l
2. seor — r o s e
3. ygar — g r a y
4. tvolei — v i o l e t
5. agemant — m a g e n t a
6. ubel — b l u e
7. oarlc — c o r a l
8. lolwey — y e l l o w

B. Start with the top box above. Write the letters on the lines to answer the riddle.

What bow cannot be tied?

a r a i n b o w

© Evan-Moor Corp. • EMC 2802 • Vocabulary Fundamentals — 135

Page 136

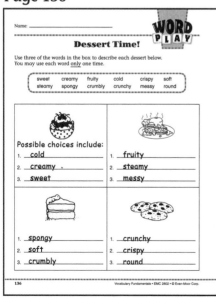

Name: _____

Dessert Time!

Use three of the words in the box to describe each dessert below. You may use each word only one time.

sweet   creamy   fruity   cold   crispy   soft
steamy   spongy   crumbly   crunchy   messy   round

Possible choices include:

1. cold
2. creamy
3. sweet

1. fruity
2. steamy
3. messy

1. spongy
2. soft
3. crumbly

1. crunchy
2. crispy
3. round

136 — Vocabulary Fundamentals • EMC 2802 • © Evan-Moor Corp.

Page 137

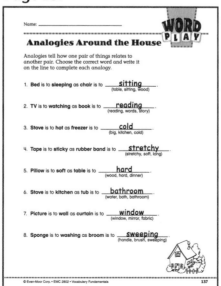

Name: _____

Analogies Around the House

Analogies tell how one pair of things relates to another pair. Choose the correct word and write it on the line to complete each analogy.

1. **Bed** is to **sleeping** as **chair** is to **sitting**
   (table, sitting, wood)

2. **TV** is to **watching** as **book** is to **reading**
   (reading, words, story)

3. **Stove** is to **hot** as **freezer** is to **cold**
   (big, kitchen, cold)

4. **Tape** is to **sticky** as **rubber band** is to **stretchy**
   (stretchy, soft, long)

5. **Pillow** is to **soft** as **table** is to **hard**
   (wood, hard, dinner)

6. **Stove** is to **kitchen** as **tub** is to **bathroom**
   (water, bath, bathroom)

7. **Picture** is to **wall** as **curtain** is to **window**
   (window, mirror, fabric)

8. **Sponge** is to **washing** as **broom** is to **sweeping**
   (handle, brush, sweeping)

© Evan-Moor Corp. • EMC 2802 • Vocabulary Fundamentals — 137

Page 138

Name: _____

Prefix Sort

Sort these blocks by matching each base word to a prefix below. Write the whole word on the line. Be sure to write words for all 12 blocks!

agree   healthy   obey
hurt   check   pay
spell   lead   kind
view   believe   behave

un–	re–
unhealthy	review
unkind	repay
unhurt	recheck
mis–	**dis–**
misspell	disagree
misbehave	disbelieve
mislead	disobey

138 — Vocabulary Fundamentals • EMC 2802 • © Evan-Moor Corp.

Page 139

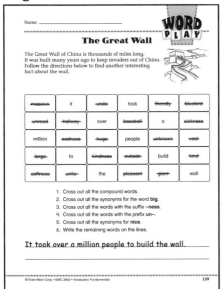

The Great Wall

The Great Wall of China is thousands of miles long. It was built many years ago to keep invaders out of China. Follow the directions below to find another interesting fact about the wall.

~~massive~~	it	~~undo~~	took	~~friendly~~	~~bluebird~~
~~unread~~	~~hallway~~	over	~~baseball~~	a	~~sickness~~
million	~~sadness~~	~~huge~~	people	~~unknown~~	~~vast~~
~~large~~	to	~~kindness~~	~~outside~~	build	~~kind~~
~~softness~~	~~untie~~	the	~~pleasant~~	~~giant~~	wall

1. Cross out all the compound words.
2. Cross out all the synonyms for the word **big**.
3. Cross out all the words with the suffix **–ness**.
4. Cross out all the words with the prefix **un–**.
5. Cross out all the synonyms for **nice**.
6. Write the remaining words on the lines.

It took over a million people to build the wall.

Page 140

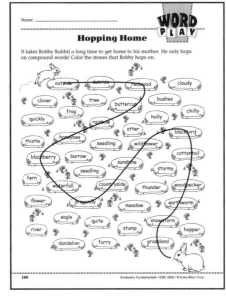

Hopping Home

It takes Robby Rabbit a long time to get home to his mother. He only hops on compound words! Color the stones that Robby hops on.

Page 141

Apple Harvest

Sort the apples into the pails by matching each base word with a suffix.
• If the word goes with the suffix **–less**, write it in the **–less** pail.
• If the word goes with **–ful**, write it in the **–ful** pail.
• Write words that can go with both suffixes in the overlapping part of the pails.

–less: end, worth, tire, sleep

–ful: help, pain, use, care, harm

both: play, forget, skill

Page 142

What has...

A. Can you find the answer to the riddle below? Use the clues to fill in the boxes. For each new word, change only the letter in the shaded box. The word you write in the last row is the answer.

Clues	k	i	c	k
to choose	p	i	c	k
you do this before you go on a trip	p	a	c	k
a good place for a picnic	p	a	r	k
not the whole thing	p	a	r	t
what a tired dog does	p	a	n	t
a piece of glass in a window	p	a	n	e
a stick used for walking	c	a	n	e
what you eat ice cream in	c	o	n	e
to arrive or enter	c	o	m	e
What has teeth but does not have a mouth?	c	o	m	b

B. Circle the picture that shows your answer.

Page 143

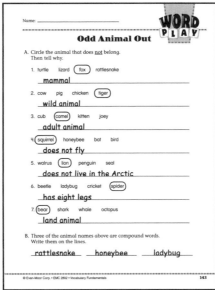

Odd Animal Out

A. Circle the animal that does **not** belong. Then tell why.

1. turtle   lizard   (fox)   rattlesnake
   mammal
2. cow   pig   chicken   (tiger)
   wild animal
3. cub   (camel)   kitten   joey
   adult animal
4. (squirrel)   honeybee   bat   bird
   does not fly
5. walrus   (lion)   penguin   seal
   does not live in the Arctic
6. beetle   ladybug   cricket   (spider)
   has eight legs
7. (bear)   shark   whale   octopus
   land animal

B. Three of the animal names above are compound words. Write them on the lines.

rattlesnake   honeybee   ladybug

Page 144

At the Produce Stand

Write three words to describe how each vegetable looks, feels, and tastes.

Answers will vary.

carrot — looks, feels, tastes
celery — looks, feels, tastes
corn — looks, feels, tastes
potato — looks, feels, tastes
onion — looks, feels, tastes
peas — looks, feels, tastes

Page 145

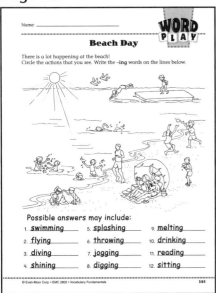

Beach Day

There is a lot happening at the beach! Circle the actions that you see. Write the **-ing** words on the lines below.

Possible answers may include:
1. swimming
2. flying
3. diving
4. shining
5. splashing
6. throwing
7. jogging
8. digging
9. melting
10. drinking
11. reading
12. sitting

Page 146

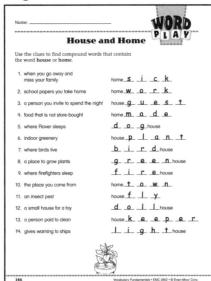

House and Home

Use the clues to find compound words that contain the word **house** or **home**.

1. when you go away and miss your family — home s i c k
2. school papers you take home — home w o r k
3. a person you invite to spend the night — house g u e s t
4. food that is not store-bought — home m a d e
5. where Rover sleeps — d o g house
6. indoor greenery — house p l a n t
7. where birds live — b i r d house
8. a place to grow plants — g r e e n house
9. where firefighters sleep — f i r e house
10. the place you come from — home t o w n
11. an insect pest — house f l y
12. a small house for a toy — d o l l house
13. a person paid to clean — house k e e p e r
14. gives warning to ships — l i g h t house

Page 147

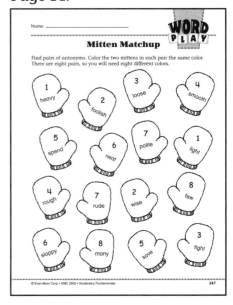

Mitten Matchup

Find pairs of antonyms. Color the two mittens in each pair the same color. There are eight pairs, so you will need eight different colors.

1 heavy
2 foolish
3 loose
4 smooth
5 spend
6 neat
7 polite
1 light
4 rough
7 rude
2 wise
8 few
6 sloppy
8 many
5 save
3 tight

Page 148

WORD PLAY

Twos and Threes

Some things just go together.
Fill in the blanks to complete each pair or trio.

1. salt and **pepper**
2. shoes and **socks**
3. lock and **key**
4. ketchup and **mustard**
5. peanut butter and **jelly**
6. macaroni and **cheese**
7. thunder and **lightning**
8. knife, fork, and **spoon**
9. red, white, and **blue**
10. morning, noon, and **night**
11. bacon, lettuce, and **tomato**
12. stop, drop, and **roll**
13. rock, paper, **scissors**
14. ready, set, **go**
15. Wynken, Blynken, and **Nod**

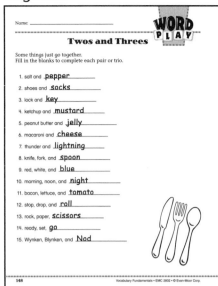

Page 149

WORD PLAY

Trees

These names of trees are missing some letters.
Use the letters in the box to fill in the blanks. You may use each letter only once. Cross off the letters as you use them.

a c d e e f h i i k l l l m m o p p r r u w

1. e **l** m
2. **f** i r
3. o a **k**
4. p **i** n e
5. p a l **m**
6. **p** e a r
7. a p p **l** e
8. **c** h **h** e r r y
9. c e d a **r**
10. b **i** r c h
11. s **p** r u c e
12. w i l l **o** **w**
13. c h **e** s t n **u** t
14. **r** e d w o o **d**

Write the letters from the box that are left over: **a** **e** **l** **m** **p**

Unscramble the letters to name another tree: **maple**

Circle the food that comes from this tree.

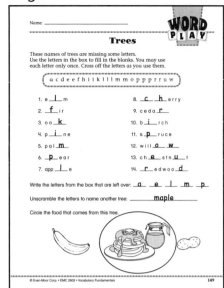

Page 150

WORD PLAY

Flower Power

Some words have many synonyms.
Fill in each flower petal with a synonym for the word in the center of the flower. **Possible answers may include:**

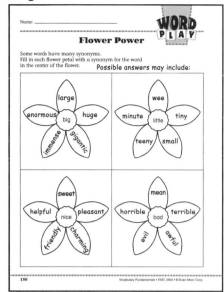

Flower 1 (big): large, huge, enormous, gigantic, immense

Flower 2 (little): wee, tiny, small, teeny, minute

Flower 3 (nice): sweet, pleasant, charming, friendly, helpful

Flower 4 (bad): mean, terrible, awful, evil, horrible

Page 151

WORD PLAY

Body Parts

Sometimes, words that are used to name body parts are also used to describe other things. For example, the mouth of a jar is the part where it opens and, just like you, an apple has a skin.

Use the words in the box to label the pictures.

legs   teeth   ear   heel   hands
neck   arms   eyes   head

teeth   **legs**   **ear**
hands   **head**   **eyes**
neck   **heel**   **arms**

Page 152

WORD PLAY

Animal Rhyme Time

Use the clues to find the two-word rhyming answers.
Examples: chubby kitty = fat cat
large hog = big pig

1. amusing rabbit — **funny** **bunny**
2. pleasant rodents — **nice** **mice**
3. dessert for a reptile — **snake** **cake**
4. two grizzlies — **bear** **pair**
5. carpet made from insects — **bug** **rug**
6. wet puppy — **soggy** **doggy**
7. hot drink for a honey-maker — **bee** **tea**
8. cozy insect — **snug** **bug**
9. poky black bird — **slow** **crow**
10. chicken yard — **hen** **pen**
11. unwell bird — **sick** **chick**
12. bath for a baby bear — **cub** **tub**

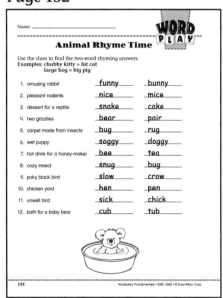

Free Sampler

Language Fundamentals

GRADE 2

What?

Language Fundamentals is your one-stop resource for focused practice on grammar, mechanics, and usage skills.

- 160 student-friendly activities, scaffolded to accommodate students' various skill levels

- Multiple-choice review pages for student assessments and standardized test preparation

- Sentence-editing pages that provide "real-world" application of skills.

Why?

- Combined with the vocabulary practice in *Vocabulary Fundamentals,* the grammar, mechanics, and usage skills covered in *Language Fundamentals* create a powerful and comprehensive resource to develop grade-level language skills.

- Once you've identified skills students are struggling with using your core language program, use the focused activities in *Language Fundamentals* for extra practice and reinforcement.

Table of Contents

Use commas to separate things in a list of three or more items.

My favorite sports are **baseball, basketball, and soccer.**
Jana, Lian, and Mori had lunch together.

Read each sentence. Add commas to separate the things in each list.

1. Samantha Chris and James went downtown.

2. They went to a clothing store a toy store and a museum.

3. Samantha bought a skirt a blouse and shoes.

4. Chris bought a shirt pants and sneakers.

5. James wanted a yo-yo a kite and a ball.

6. They ate sandwiches carrots and applesauce for lunch.

7. Samantha brought her wallet glasses and a book.

8. Chris had pencils markers and paper in his backpack.

9. They saw mummies fossils and models of dinosaurs at the museum.

10. The children their parents and the teachers had fun.

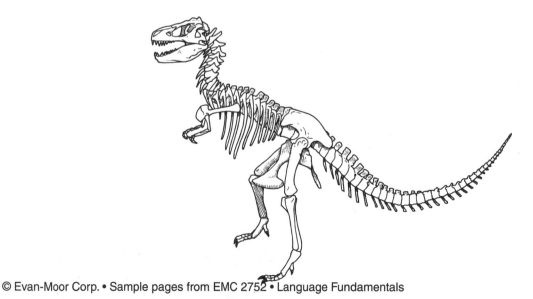

> Use a comma between the day and the year in a date.
>
> Julio's grandfather was born on August **23, 1957**.

Write the sentences correctly. Add commas where they belong.

1. My grandparents were married on June 6 1972.

   _____

   _____

2. My mother was born on September 20 1973.

   _____

   _____

3. My mother and father met on May 6 1993.

   _____

   _____

4. They got married on March 3 1995.

   _____

   _____

5. I was born on July 4 1998.

   _____

   _____

Name _____

> When you address an envelope, use a comma between the city and state in an address.
>
> Mrs. Janelle Washington
> 422 Main Street
> **New Orleans, Louisiana** 10100

Add commas where needed in these addresses.

1. Samuel Irving
   231 Hollywood Boulevard
   Los Angeles California 90007

2. Mary Jefferson
   18 Broadway
   Atlanta Georgia 30703

3. Juan Gomez
   31 Donceles St.
   Santa Fe New Mexico 86505

4. Annie Martin
   651 Central Parkway
   Austin Texas 78707

5. Evan Harper
   123 Lincoln Street
   Evanston Illinois 60903

6. Julia Osborne
   789 Merrimac Street
   Newburyport Massachusetts 05950

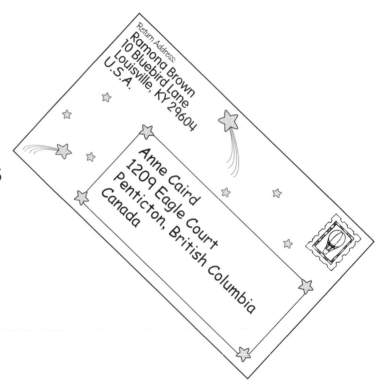

Name _____

Fill in the bubble next to the correct answer.

1. Which sentence is written correctly?
   Ⓐ Maria likes mangoes bananas, and coconuts.
   Ⓑ Ryan likes apples, oranges, and grapes,
   Ⓒ Ryan likes peppers potatoes and lettuce.
   Ⓓ Maria likes corn, peas, and broccoli.

2. Which sentence is written correctly?
   Ⓐ Ji Sun hops, skips, and runs.
   Ⓑ Manuel reads writes, and draws pictures.
   Ⓒ Laurel sits rests and sleeps.
   Ⓓ Fleur draws paints and, writes.

3. Which date is written correctly?
   Ⓐ December, 1 1969
   Ⓑ November 13, 2003
   Ⓒ April 18 2010
   Ⓓ September, 19, 1988

4. Which date is written correctly?
   Ⓐ I was born on October 15 2000.
   Ⓑ My mother was born on June, 15 1975.
   Ⓒ My friend was born on August 11, 2001.
   Ⓓ My father was born on December, 6, 1973.

5. Which address is written correctly?
   Ⓐ San Francisco California,
   Ⓑ Cleveland Ohio
   Ⓒ Detroit. Michigan
   Ⓓ Dallas, Texas

Name _____

Correct these sentences.

1. We had flour salt and sugar.

_____

_____

2. We needed eggs milk and raisins

_____

_____

3. The date on the milk was June 2 2006.

_____

_____

4. We were baking on June 7 2006.

_____

_____

5. We made new milk with powder water and a whisk.

_____

_____

6. We made another cake on August 23 2006.

_____

_____